Finding Freedom
Was Just the Beginning

Sherry Ward with Shari Ho

Finding Freedom Was Just the Beginning

God's Hand in the Journey

Published by Square Tree Publishing
www.SquareTreePublishing.com
ISBN-13: 978-1-7329587-0-8

FIRST EDITION

Cover Design: Cathy Arkle—The Thumbprint group
Interior Format: Cheri Lasota
Author Photo: Melody Welch
Line Editing: Monica Bosque
Cover Photo: Ben Beason
Content Editing: Melodie Fox

For more information, please contact: info@squaretreepublishing.com

For bulk orders of 10 books or more, contact:

Square Tree Publishing at info@squaretreepublishing.com

Square Tree Disclaimer

The story you are about to read is based upon the true-life events of Ho Hsiao-feng, aka 'Shari Ho'. This narrative includes her memories, to the best of her recollection, as a young native Paiwan child of Taiwan, being sold as a slave, her abuse at the hands of her captors, both in Taiwan and the United States, and her subsequent escape and life in the United States.

The names have been changed to protect the privacy of those involved in the surrounding events. In no way is this story written to place blame or to single out those who played a part in Shari being sold as a slave or in her mistreatment, nor is it intended for her or others to profit from these events, but rather to shine a light on the plight of human trafficking survivors and the crime of human trafficking that still exists today. This story is meant to promote awareness and to encourage those who suspect a person is involved in the crime of human trafficking to speak out about such suspected activity; and to teach forgiveness and healing to survivors of such crimes, and to bring healing to all.

Dedication—Sherry Ward

I dedicate this book to God, who is bigger than we can even imagine. As we lay down our own agenda and let Him accomplish His—that is when miracles happen!

Dedication—Shari Ho

I dedicate this book to God, because he has always been there for me even, through all the hard times.

He has helped me to find forgiveness, which is true freedom.

Table of Contents

Section III – Back Home

Recommendations

"I've seen the extreme depths of misery and pinnacle of joy in my experiences in law enforcement. I've not seen a better encapsulation of both than in this book."

—Special Agent, Homeland Security Investigations

"No matter how interesting a story may be, there is something equally intriguing about what happens behind the scenes. *Finding Freedom Was Just the Beginning* is that backstory, the behind-the-scenes parallel plot of all those who were there to help Shari navigate the tricky years after she was freed from domestic slavery. The star of this backstage show? God. We learn of His mind-bending, mysterious, clever, comforting, and constant presence in the process to get Shari's story told through the endearing and conversational narrative of Shari's friend, mentor, protector, and chauffeur: Sherry Ward. Sherry is both humble and trusting in God's plan, even when she had no idea where He was leading her, for as we know that while we plan, God laughs. Sherry was smart enough to see what He had in mind first...

Read *Finding Freedom Was Just the Beginning*; it will renew even the weariest of spirits and challenge the cynic. You will laugh, cry, and be inspired by the elegant presence of God in our everyday moments."

—Brenda Wells, Founder i-5 Freedom Network

Brand stands ū values
 integrity
1. Specialization - one area of achievement
2. Leadership -
3. Personality - In all aspects - including flaw
4. Distinctiveness - sign Name, Dress in style
5. visibility - show business
           Networking
6. utility - Behind scenes match public
7. Persistence - ignore fads
8. Good Will - Back from the future thinking

First thing people do is
check your reputation

6 Personality Traits you need to be a Successful
                Brian Tracy   Entrepreneur

Have potential to radically improve world

• Love what you do
• Take productive actions
• Define Business goals and come up with detailed
    Plans to achieve them
• Remain flexible
• Be honest
• Have Emotional Intelligence
    Be sensitive to Employees emotions

Branding - The promoting of a
product of service
by identifying
it with a
particular
brand

A marketing practice in which
a company creates a name,
symbol or design that is
easily identifiable as
belonging to the company.
This helps to identify a product
and distinguish it from other
products & services.

human beings decide emotionally
& Justify logically

PREFACE

I own a company called Square Tree Publishing. When I first started the company, I struggled finding my 'why' for the company. I went to a branding meeting with a guy named Brad.

"What do you really want?" Brad asked.

"I don't know," I hesitantly answered.

"Well, that's why we are here, to figure it out and find the core of who you are as a company and be able to articulate it," he said confidently.

After four hours of intense questioning and refinement, we reached our answer.

Our core value is…Your Message Matters!

For every author that came to us, they needed a message that mattered and one that we could amplify for the world to hear. We finally arrived at the central value of our company, Square Tree Publishing.

It felt good.

It felt right.

It resonated with who we were as a company.

But with that new revelation, came a set of new issues to be reconciled.

In the beginning, in order to get the company going, we had many authors sign on who may not have fit this new core value.

I had numerous authors come to me, and because I was new, I took everyone as a client. The only issue with taking on anyone was a lot of their messages did not matter to us. Many did not line up entirely with our core values as a company.

When your core belief is, 'Your Message Matters,'—yet obviously it does not—it feels disingenuous and does not resonate with us.

I began questioning God.

I began to ask Him questions about who we were to bring on board as Square Tree authors.

It was during this time when I was at a women's conference at my church, when this new core value came full circle.

I began a quiet conversation with the Lord as I walked around outside in the patio.

I asked God two very specific questions that night:

"Whose message matters to You?"

"Who are we supposed to promote their message?"

There are many people who have tremendous messages that matter, but the second question was key. Were we the company that was to champion their message?

Immediately, before I could even get that last question out of my mouth, I felt God point out a young short Asian gal in the courtyard and I felt Him say, "Tell her story. Her story matters!"

I heard it in my spirit as clear as a deaf person hearing for the first time.

I gathered my courage and walked up to her and said, "Hi, my name is Sherry."

She replied, "Hi, my name is Shari, too!"

We began talking about her story and I absolutely knew that this is what I had prayed about and that Shari's message mattered. This unknown young girl who had been a slave for twenty years—that girl—that was the girl whose message mattered to God, and most importantly, we were the team to champion her message. Unbeknownst to me at the time, Shari was also praying that God would send her the right person to tell her story.

It was not always smooth sailing. One of the first phone calls I received was from Shari's earthly guardian angel named Sister Marianna. She grilled me like a well-done hamburger on a hot summer day about my intentions and what I wanted to do with Shari's story. The entire time I had a smile on my face, not because it was an easy conversation, but because I knew that Shari had an advocate, someone who cared enough about her to question the intentions of someone new coming into her life. I loved it! I knew she was in great hands with Sister Marianna at the helm.

Shari had several other offers throughout the years from different people and organizations to write a book about her harrowing story, but she later told me they never seemed like the right fit. When I met Shari, it took nearly a year to gain her trust and to allow us to tell her story. It was absolutely worth the wait. She had been so abused that trust was a rare commodity, and one I did not take lightly in working with her.

This four-and-a-half-year book journey has been one big God-adventure through and through, with many nights of crying out to God, "When God…when…when will the book be done?"

It has taken a lot longer than anticipated, due to the extensive research that the writer, Melodie Fox, had to do. Melodie's heart is to get the story just right, and to be true, not only to Shari, but to Shari's family, the Taiwanese culture, and most importantly, her tribal township.

This book, *Finding Freedom Was Just the Beginning*, will take you behind the scenes of this incredible journey of the making of this book, and how God showed up in big ways throughout the process. I believe God will use Shari's story not only to shift national norms, but to impact all the nations around it.

Our hope is that by reading this book, you will get a sense of how God is in our midst even through the most horrible of circumstances, and how God can redeem any situation. Shari is not just a human trafficked survivor—she is a thriver. She is growing every day in her relationship with God and is learning the common things in life we take for granted every day.

Our prayer is that you will be encouraged in your own life to know that truly nothing is impossible with God, and that what He has done for Shari, He can do, and even more, for you.

*"Jesus looked at them and said,
'With man this is impossible,
but with God all things are possible.'"*
—Matthew 19:26

ACKNOWLEDGEMENTS

Shari Ho

There are so many who have helped me along the way, not only to be where I am today, but to see that my story was written. All of them have become good friends, and some I now call my family; your names have been changed to protect your privacy, but nothing can change how much you mean to me. Thank you so much!

Cindy

Thank you so much for coming to Taiwan with us and preparing all the travel arrangements. You are awesome! We could not have done the trip without you.

Melodie

Thank you for coming to Taiwan. I loved how you went to the day market with me and helped me cook. I will always remember you talking into your phone the whole trip. You are so funny!

Sherry Ward

My Family

I thank my God for my amazing family, who has stood by me as I have pursued what I have felt God wanted me to do. Thanks to my husband who has worked tirelessly to support me through these God-adventures and my children who have grown up to follow their own God-adventures.

Cindy

You were the glue that held our trip together from the very beginning. Your calm manner in the face of tough challenges on the trip will be forever remembered. We needed you on the trip and I thank God that you followed His voice to go.

Melodie

Thank you for pushing me to go on the Taiwan trip. Even though I was dragging my heels at the beginning, it was one of the most memorable trips I have ever taken to date. I will be forever grateful for your insistence that we go to Taiwan.

THE STORY

"It takes a village to raise a child, but it takes an entire community to save one."

—Sherry Ward

Shari grew up in Dawu Township in southern Taiwan. She was born the second child of six sisters and three brothers into a large indigenous Paiwan family. Being the second born, it was natural for her to be very protective of her sisters. With her small stature, she had the fortitude and persistence of a girl twice her size. Ever since she was young, she had been fierce when it came to standing up for what was right. It would take years to get that fighter spirit to come out again after her twenty years of slavery, but it was there and laid dormant for years.

Shari's family was very poor and her father began selling the sisters, or 'adopting' them out as they liked to call it, for money to survive. Her father was violent at times, mostly due to his heavy drinking. No one was immune to his anger, not even Shari's mother, who he once pushed forcefully, causing her to tumble down a hillside.

Shari loved to go out into the local fields behind her house and pick flowers with her mom and sisters. Maybe it was a reprieve from the harsh reality at home with her father. It was a complicated family filled with a history of reasons why everyone acted the way they did. Nonetheless, it was still home for Shari.

When Shari had just turned seven years old, or so she believes, because they never really celebrated birthdays, she was with her family one night when her mother began cooking a large meal which was unusual, since most nights they barely had anything to eat. Shari's mother, knowing there was never enough food, always ate last. Meat was rarely eaten, for it was hard to come by. They all loved rice, which they seldom had, but more often they ate a type of porridge which was their typical dinner. However, on this night, something was different. All the sisters began cutting up the vegetables and preparing the food. They all sat together around the table, which was also quite unusual for them. For the first time, Shari could remember the delicious smell of chicken cooking along with rice, steaming away in a large pot on the stove.

"Do you know why we are having this big meal with chicken and rice?" Shari's mother announced.

"It is because your older sister is working hard and this money she has earned has bought this feast for all of us," she continued.

Shari's heart was so full of joy at the thought of all of her family eating together. She did not know this would be the last meal she would ever eat with her family. This was the last time she would laugh and eat and feel full inside. It would be twenty years until she again would lay eyes on most of those in the room that night.

As Shari bit into the chicken it tasted bitter, for the herb surrounding it touched her lips. "Mama, something is wrong here," she said. "The chicken is no good. It is spoiling the meal," Shari announced, disappointedly.[1]

Shari's mom was serious and seemed a bit sad. Shari had not seen this look before.

After a moment, Shari's mom spoke, but Shari did not expect the answer she gave. "Life is like this meal. It is sweet and good, but bitter and hard. Your life will be like this, too. Always be patient; endure and overcome because tomorrow will always be better. Beneath the bitter herb is tender meat, to make you strong. Do not stop at the first bite; keep eating. Tomorrow will be better. You must remember this meal. You must remember this night. And, remember my words when times seems too bitter to bear. Keep yourself strong with this thought."

Shari's family all ate, and the meal was good, but there was something different about this night. Shari knew things were never to be the same, although she was not quite sure why. But

---

1   Excerpts from *My Name is Also Freedom*

she always remembered what her mother had taught her that night. She closed her eyes, taking a picture in her mind of that evening. She was determined to remember it; to remember what her mother had taught her that night.

Shari had been sold.

The next day Shari was driven far away into the city of Taipei to live with a family and become their personal house servant. She was to care for an older woman, The Old Lady, who eventually immigrated to the United States with her family. It was not until twenty years later that Shari found the courage through a Good Samaritan to run away from this life of indentured servitude.

Shari Ho's full story is found in the book, *My Name is Also Freedom* by Melodie Fox.

 BACKSTORY

While Shari was a slave and living in Taipei, her father passed away. She had mixed feeling with her father's passing. She had anger that he had sold her, yet wanted the love that only a father can give his daughter. The Old Lady allowed her to go to the funeral, but not to stay for the family gathering afterwards. She quickly pulled her away when the funeral was over and that was the last time she saw any of her family for over a decade.

SECTION I

PRE-TRIP

"Blessed are the pure in heart,
for they shall see God."

—Matthew 5:8

THE TRANSLATOR

"I do not want to go!" I proclaimed.

"You go on without me," I continued saying to Melodie Fox, the writer of Shari Ho's story.

I was so busy with my other projects that I just did not feel like I had the time to go overseas, let alone have the finances for the trip.

The whole idea of going to Taiwan started when I was introduced to a young lady named Beatrice who went to school with my daughter. Beatrice is a Mandarin Chinese translator for a large church. I was thrilled that we had found an interpreter because we wanted to translate Shari's book into Mandarin.

"Wow, what are the odds?" I thought to myself.

"She is even Taiwanese," an added bonus, I thought.

I invited Beatrice out to breakfast with her unofficial adopted American 'dad' who used to be a professor in Taipei. It was a wonderful conversation and Beatrice said that we needed to visit Taiwan. The minute she said these words, there was something imparted into our spirit.

It was like she was Obi-Wan Kenobi in Star Wars as we all repeated back to her what she said, "We need to go to Taiwan."

After that conversation I spent a lot of time trying to coordinate with Beatrice's schedule so that she could come with the team to Taiwan.

Melodie absolutely knew we should go.

Me?

Well, I wasn't so sure.

Melodie insisted that I needed to be on the trip, but to be honest, I was not excited to go. Interestingly enough, Beatrice was never able to go with us. I was not sure how we were going to travel the country without using an interpreter. Shari knew the language, but did not know how to read or write very well in either Mandarin or English.

Then a woman named Cindy came to my mind. She, along with some other friends, befriended Shari when she regained her freedom. They taught her English and a lot of other skills we take for granted every day in America. Shari had to learn for the first time how to use money, take the bus…all the practical things we need to function in the world around us.

It was during this time that I had a question for Cindy about an entirely different issue, and so I called to ask her about it.

While I was dialing the phone, I was rehearsing in my mind what I would say to her.

"Hi, my name is Sherry and I own a company called Square Tree Publishing…you may not remember me…but I am working with Shari on her autobiography," and so the chatter went on in my head.

I had met Cindy a couple of times before, but I was not sure if she would remember who I was.

Ring…ring…ring…then a voice.

"Hi Sherry, I was expecting your call," she said as she answered the phone.

Dumbfounded, the line went quiet.

"Well…ah…oh…hello," I said, trying to make sense of her greeting.

"How did you know I was going to call?" I asked her.

"I just had this sense from God that you were going to call," she said matter-of-factly.

We proceeded to talk about the question I had originally called her about, and then I blurted out, "Would you like to go to Taiwan with us?"

"Somehow, I knew you were going to ask me that," she stated very calmly.

Cindy was already thinking about going to Taiwan to visit her relatives and to do work with a church overseas, so it was pretty good timing. 'Pretty good' because it was not exactly when she wanted to take her trip.

After the course of a couple weeks, we talked several times trying to coordinate the timing of the trip to fit Cindy's schedule while trying to get good pricing on the flights. We finally came up with the dates that would work with everyone's schedule, including Shari's daycare business.

It was now official...Cindy was part of the Square Tree team going to Taiwan. The logistics still needed to be worked out, but she would be our translator and tour guide while we were there. Little did we know at the time how important Cindy would be on the team, especially for our safety.

Cindy coordinated all of our travel arrangements, along with booking all the buses, trains, and airplanes we needed for the journey. She even reserved all of our Airbnb's for the trip as well. What I did not quite realize until we landed in the country is that we had no agenda. I kept saying, tongue-in-cheek, that we were going on a God-adventure. I had no idea how foretelling that statement would be on the trip. This was going to be a God-trip from the very beginning. No agenda…no meetings scheduled…only following God's lead as we moved from city to city. And oh, what a God-trip it was!

 BACKSTORY

Cindy was such a God-send and one of the most levelheaded members of our team, which was very much needed when the police were called on us while we were in Taiwan. Long story…but suffice to say, Cindy is excellent in a time of crisis. You definitely want her on your team.

THE PLANNING

During the course of the next couple months we began planning our trip—or so I thought. Cindy began researching Airbnbs in our destination cities where we were going and figuring out how many days we would be at each city. What I didn't realize is that we never actually planned what we were going to do while we were there.

I kept saying aloud, "This trip is one big God-adventure."

I did not realize at the time how prophetic that statement would become.

As we began planning the trip, I asked each member of the Square Tree team what they wanted out of the trip so that we could accomplish as many things as we could on our list. For Melodie, who was writing Shari's story, it was all about being with Shari as much as possible. She wanted to see how Shari responded to the different places that we saw, and to capture her emotions from that time in her life as a slave. Melodie wanted to 'walk in her shoes' so that she could translate that feeling into the book. Melodie's heart was also to understand the Taiwanese culture in order to make sure the book was authentic and real.

Cindy's desire was to help us in translating signs, talking to taxi cab drivers, and interpreting in meetings we attended. She also wanted to visit her in-laws while we were there.

For me, I wanted to meet other Taiwanese publishers and begin a business relationship in order to get an international foreign rights deal for Shari's book. I wanted to see Shari's book translated into Mandarin Chinese and published in Taiwan with a larger publisher. After reading many cultural books, I knew that it was all about building a relationship and not necessarily getting a deal the same day of the meeting. Little did I know at the time what God was about to do to get Shari's book in Taiwan.

Shari had a list a mile long, which she kept texting me for weeks, adding to her list! I had to laugh every time I got a new text of something else she wanted to do in Taiwan. She wanted to go to the night markets, which we ended up doing on a regular basis. Her favorite thing to do was buy chicken feet and chicken hearts and liver which she ate on a stick like some sort of corn on the cob back home. None of us partook in this 'feast', but Shari sure liked it!

One of the things Shari really wanted to do was go to Alishan Mountain. It is a very famous mountain where the Taiwanese go to see the sunrise. It was completely out of the way on our trip, yet I knew it was important to Shari, so I made a way to fit it into our plans. While we were getting ready for our trip, Cindy was very specific that we should pack light. I think Melodie was the only one that really heeded her advice. I brought an oversized bag because of all the gifts I brought, and Shari brought three bags that were so big you could hardly see her standing behind them.

The most important thing on Shari's list was to see her mom. The previous time she went to Taiwan she was prevented from seeing her mom and this was one of the most important things to her on this trip because her mom was getting old and had a slow growing cancer. We made sure we planned to visit the Dawu Township so that we could arrange a trip to see her mom.

The last thing on Shari's wish list was to go to all the places where she was held as a slave. It sounds very depressing, but it could not be further from the truth, as you'll see later on.

"How in the world was I going to make sure that everyone got what they wanted out of the trip?" I mused.

That remained to be seen, but as we continued to plan, things came into focus. At least we knew where were staying and which cities we would visit.

I kept saying, "This is going to be a God-adventure," simply because it took the pressure off me to make everything happen on this trip. How could I know at the time, just how much of an adventure God had planned for us?

With the planning now in full swing, there was no way I could back out and not go to Taiwan. With each day that passed, Cindy's value on the team became more and more evident and we realized that there was no way we could have done the trip without her and we had not even taken off from the airport yet!

 BACKSTORY

Sometimes we go into situations with our feet dragging and Taiwan was one of those times for me. God was sneaky in getting me to go, because my administrative skills kicked into high gear, and by then it was too late for me to back out of the trip. I was fully committed. I have traveled all over the world, and it was one of the most profound trips to date that I have ever taken!

THE AIRPORT

"Shari you need to come with us to the airport," I pushed as strongly as I could on our last team Skype meeting.

"No, Sherry, I want to go with my husband because there are so many memories and triggers that come back to me going to the airport. I want to go with him!" she exclaimed.

I pushed as strongly as I could until Shari broke down and started crying.

"Okay," I conceded. "Meet us at the airport."

The day finally arrived, and all of our bags were packed. All of the Square Tree team, except for Shari, met at my house with plenty of time to spare, just in case we ran into traffic.

Once we arrived at the airport, we navigated the new airport kiosks which were a bit tricky, but we were able to get through them. Then we went up to our gate to wait for our boarding. We called Shari, but she did not answer her phone. We began to worry when Cindy got a text saying Shari was stuck in traffic because there was an accident.

"Boarding Flight 778 bound for Taipei," announced the China Airline attendant over the loud speaker in her heavy accent.

We made our way to the line to begin boarding, frantically texting Shari for updates where she was on the road.

The line continued to shrink as I began to get a sinking feeling in my stomach while a voice in my head said, "Shari is not going to make the flight."

Shari was still not there. Panicking, I called her again to see if she had entered the airport circle yet. I could not tell the airline attendant to hold the flight until I knew she was at least on the bottom floor of the airport.

"Final boarding call for all passengers to board flight 778," came the announcement. But Shari was still not in the building, she had just entered the airport circle, possibly another twenty minutes away.

With all of our emotions heightened with anticipation of what was coming, we mustered up the strength to continue in the line as we approached the air bridge entrance and airplane door.

The line of people to board the aircraft was shrinking faster than I wanted. If there was ever a time in my life when I wanted a line to take forever it was now.

Finally, our team was the last in line to board. By that time, Shari called us to say she was downstairs trying to use the kiosk to get her boarding ticket and no one would help her. Shari was completely melting down in tears trying to log into the kiosk. Shari's reading and writing skills were limited, so the kiosk was very challenging for her to navigate. I know how challenging it was for our team to figure out the kiosk and we all have college degrees!

"It's too late. She won't make the flight," the check-in attendant firmly said.

"But can you just bring her up? No one is helping her downstairs," I frantically said, trying to figure out how I was going to fix this situation, as the full weight of being the CEO came on me.

"You have to board now," the attendant said in a stern intimidating voice.

"I cannot board this flight!" I said in the firmest voice I could muster.

"You do not have a choice. We have already boarded your luggage," she retorted angrily.

Cindy and I walked up to the counter and explained to the attendant Shari's situation and told the one-minute abridged version. Yes—we played the human trafficking card. It was the only thing left we could do. The male flight attendant was kind, but the lady flight attendant was not going to have her passengers be late on her flight and get in trouble from her supervisors.

I had to make a decision.

Do I get on board that flight and coach Shari from the sidelines on the phone to help her get on the next flight or do I stay behind to help her. I was never one for being on the sidelines, anyway!

It was not really a question. I already knew what I was going to do. My gut was telling me that if I did not stay behind, Shari would not come to Taiwan on her own. The only logical answer was for me to stay behind. Cindy knew the language and could help Melodie in the country. I knew instinctively that if I did not stay back, Shari would not make it to Taiwan by herself, especially in the condition she was in.

I told the flight attendant my decision to stay. I was honestly taking a gamble that she would bring Shari up from the kiosk on the first floor, rather than deboarding my luggage. My gamble did not pay off as I watched them call to the baggage handlers to unload my luggage. I was shocked at how fast they took off my bags!

I had no grand plan now, except to go downstairs and help Shari. She was crying and very upset for being late and missing the flight. I went straight into 'fix it' mode. We talked to the flight attendants...the same attendants that were upstairs; some nice, and one that honestly did not like her job!

I reached out to the male attendant because he seemed to really care about our situation the most. He told me the next flight was in twelve hours and that the flight was full. I began to pray under my breath that we would get on that flight. I spoke to a supervisor and she said that they would put us on the wait list, and we needed to come back four hours later and wait in line all over again to see if we could get on that flight.

Not the greatest news, but at least we knew what we had to do to try and get on the next flight. Now onto my next concern...calming Shari down.

I love to listen to podcasts and it just so happened that I had listened to one the day before from a guy who had such horrific things happen to him; he almost lost his life. His advice to all the listeners was to feel the negative emotion for five minutes and then to let it go. You allow yourself five minutes to 'feel the feeling', and then you move on. I decided to try this with Shari. She kept apologizing over and over for being late and finally I said,

"Okay, you have five minutes to feel bad and get upset at yourself for being late. After the five minutes is over, I do not want to hear about it anymore."

It worked!!!

She tried a couple times to go back to feeling bad about being late, but I kept telling her that her five minutes were over. I even made up a little hand sign to go with it and that made it more of a lighthearted time. I took my fingers and closed them together, made a pulling down gesture right in front of my face. The gesture seemed funny, but what a powerful tool and it worked so well.

Shari kept saying over and over, "Why aren't you mad?"

I think I went into 'fix it' mode, so anger just was not an option at the time. This technique became a catalyst in Shari's life. In times where she is tempted to get angry, she is reminded of that day at the airport. Sometimes we joke, and I will do my hand signal with her and it works every time. She will still mention the airport incident to this day. We always hear about God turning something bad around for the good, but this was one case I saw it firsthand and it has had a lasting effect. God used that day at the airport to cement our relationship.

After four hours we went back in line, and the curt female attendant talked to us again, but I firmly dismissed her as the male attendant was truly helping us. Somehow, he was able to get us on the next flight even though it was a full flight.

He told me to go to the counter to pick up my tickets. We waited in line yet again. When it was finally our turn, we walked up to the counter.

"That will be $600," the lady at the counter said, matter-of-factly.

"Why is it $600?" I said, trying to keep a straight face so that I did not give away my true feelings.

"There is a fee for changing your flight, and in addition, you are booking a premium flight because it is at night," she continued.

Normally I would try and talk my way out of the $600 charge, but I knew in my heart it was futile—besides, I was just thankful that we got on the flight. I gulped really hard as I pulled out my credit card and said under my breath, "I trust you God." To be honest, I really did not have any choice *but* to trust God.

I took Shari to dinner at the Hard Rock Cafe inside the airport and I was being silly on purpose to get her to laugh and lighten the mood. I was thankful when she began to get excited about going to Taiwan again. When we planned the trip, we had decided that every day we were on our trip we would post a Facebook Live @mynameisalsofreedom about our time together. During dinner Shari and I posted our very first Facebook Live video of our adventure so far. On the FB Live post, I put a link to Shari's GoFundMe campaign to raise money for the additional $600 that we had to pay for the flight.

After a couple hours I began to feel God speaking to my heart, "Do you trust me to repay you for the money you spent for the new tickets?"

"Take down the GoFundMe link at the top of your FB post," I felt Him say to me.

I did what I felt led to do, but I was not too happy about it. I made myself say, "I trust you God." I was letting my obedience rule me—not my feelings over the issue; it was truly a faith walk.

❧ BACKSTORY ❧

Two days later I received a text from one of the ladies I work with. She said, "You will not believe this, but we just had $800 in orders come through today!" I fell on my knees and thanked God for his complete provision even with the GoFundMe link gone. I had taken the GoFundMe link off the post, but forgot it was still on the Facebook About Page. Another $100 donation come through that link as well. Wow! God is amazing! My faith grew tremendously that day. I did not know at the time just how significant that experience was going to be as I was faced with another financial need a few days later that was twenty times that amount. God knew I needed this experience to be able to stand in faith for what was about to come.

SECTION II

TAIWAN

"He brought me out into a spacious place; he rescued me because he delighted in me."

—Psalm 18:19

THE ARRIVAL

Shari and I made it to Taiwan twenty-three hours later. Exhausted, but excited to finally be in the country, Cindy texted us to look for a man in a car that would take us to our Airbnb where we were staying. When the man pulled up, I kept looking at him and looking at my phone to make sure it was the right guy. I did not want to drive away in the car with the wrong guy! The driver dropped us off right in the middle of town with bustling traffic in what looked like an Asian farmers market.

"Is this the right place?" I requested Shari to ask him.

"Yes, I think so," the driver said in Mandarin.

The driver did not sound too convincing, but he dropped us off in the middle of the market anyway with Shari's huge luggage in tow. Shari, a small statured gal, was pushing a suitcase which came up to her waist along with two other big bags she was carrying. I tried to wrestle her for her bags, but she was independent and did not want the help.

"With all those bags, was she permanently staying in Taiwan?" I thought to myself.

We walked down this market place that looked like it was straight out of a Jackie Chan movie. If there was ever a time in my travels that screamed *tourist,* this yelled it all the way down the street. We must have looked ridiculous navigating our way through all those vendors and shoppers with all our luggage.

Meat hanging from hooks—with the heads intact—and unique smells rising from outdoor cooking, I knew I was in a completely different culture. The market was bustling with young and old alike, buying their vegetables, meat, toys, and clothing all in the same place. We squeezed through the back of two street vendors and came to a door that led to a flat several floors above. We struggled to get all of our luggage up the winding uneven, narrow staircase, one bag at a time, until we reached the third floor. I guess they did not believe in elevators! We had finally united with Melodie and Cindy one full day after we were separated at the airport.

As we walked in the door, Shari became really quiet. I knew this meant she was processing something that she had been through when she was little. We later found out that this flat looked exactly like the one she used to stay in with The Old Lady. It had the same type of rooms—even a set of bunkbeds—just like The Old Lady's house. This time however, Shari was free and no longer had to sleep on the ground with a ragged old blanket with no pillow. This time, she had a bed to sleep in and had the freedom to do anything she wanted to do in Taiwan. It was a healing experience. Shari would have many similar encounters of being in some of those dark places and finding healing from her past.

As we settled into our Airbnb, Cindy began immediately emailing and calling a few publishers we had researched before we left the U.S. I wanted a deal with a big publisher. I truly wanted Shari's story to be shared around the world and I felt like a big publisher would have the capacity to do that. God had something greater in store for us that we were not expecting.

Cindy emailed different Taiwanese publishers letting them know who we were, that we were in Taiwan, and she asked for a meeting. One of the publishers we had researched I was really excited about because they were doing some cutting-edge stories in the Asian market, but they turned us down for a meeting. Many of them did not want to meet us, except one—Elim Publishing. They said they may have fifteen minutes for us to talk to an assistant in the company. Even if it was only fifteen minutes, we would take that meeting. We were thrilled!

Cindy told them 'yes' and she set up a meeting for us the following day.

That evening I could not sleep very well because of the jet lag. I got up at 3:00 a.m. and I felt God telling me that Elim was our publisher and that we were supposed to partner with them. I kept seeing the number 555, feeling it was a sign, even before I left for Taiwan, and God had given me a verse in Isaiah to go with it.

"Surely you will summon nations you know not,
and nations you do not know will come running
to you, because of the Lord your God, the Holy
One of Israel, for he has endowed you with
splendor."
—Isaiah 55:5

So while everyone was still asleep, I began declaring this over the nation.

I had a feeling that something big was about to happen! I had no idea just how big.

❧ BACKSTORY ❧

We did not know that Elim Publishing was also a church that had many different book stores and worked with well-known Christian authors all over the world, translating their books. We got way more than we bargained for that day at Elim.

THE NUMBERS

"**B**eep—beep—beep," went the alarm as I hit the snooze, trying to find the energy to get up. After a few minutes, I peeked over my covers and saw that the clock read 5:55 a.m. "There it is again!" I thought to myself.

Weeks before we had planned for this trip, the number 555 or some sort of a combination of 5's kept coming up over and over. I drove to church one day on the freeway and off to my right was a pink office building with the address 5555. Sometimes I would look down at my cell phone and it would say 5:55 p.m.

Finally, one day I asked, "Okay, God, what's up with all the 5's?"

I knew that the number 5 usually represents grace. Was He trying to show me that we had grace to go to Taiwan? I felt led to pick up my Bible and read Isaiah 55:5.

Whoaaa! I had my answer.

> *"Surely you will summon nations you know not,*
> *and nations you do not know will come running*
> *to you, because of the Lord your God, the Holy*
> *One of Israel, for he has endowed you with*
> *splendor."*
>
> —Isaiah 55:5

I felt like we had favor with an entire nation that we knew nothing about. I was at the helm of three major flagship programs for Square Tree Publishing at that time. I felt God had given me a verse for the other programs, and now I had a verse for Shari Ho's book as well.

One of the flagship programs at Square Tree Publishing is a program called *Hurting Moms, Mending Hearts,* designed for moms who have teenagers or adult children who are making self-destructive choices and creating community through support groups. The verse God had given me for that program is in the book of Isaiah.

> *"Surely the islands look to me; in the lead are the*
> *ships of Tarshish, bringing your children from*
> *afar, with their silver and gold, to the honor of*
> *the Lord your God, the Holy One of Israel, for he*
> *has endowed you with splendor."*
>
> —Isaiah 60:9

The sister program of Hurting Moms is called *Grieving Moms, Finding Hope*. It is for moms who have lost a child in death, and creating community through support groups. The Scripture I felt the Lord give me for that program is also in Isaiah.

> *"Provide for those who grieve in Zion—to bestow on them a crown of beauty instead of ashes, the oil of joy instead of mourning, and a garment of praise instead of a spirit of despair. They will be called oaks of righteousness, a planting of the Lord for the display of his splendor."*
> —Isaiah 61:3

If you look at these two verses, and now this third verse in Isaiah 55:5 for Shari Ho's book, they all end with the same words—'for he has endowed you with splendor.'

I asked a friend who knows how to read Hebrew what the word 'splendor' means. In Hebrew, each letter is a picture and it also corresponds to a number. When you break down the pictures in the word splendor, it means, "Because you humbled yourself and spoke with the Father first, He will glorify you and He will be glorified."

If you look at the Hebrew numbers, the Hebrew word splendor represents the number 80. Moses was 80 years old when he led the people in a mass exodus out of slavery. When you read this same word represented by the number it means,

'Because you spoke with the Father and asked; there will be a great exodus for a new beginning for many.'

That is exactly what we are believing for in Shari Ho's story. We have prayed to God and asked that there will be a great exodus for a new beginning for many victims of human trafficking.

God is getting ready to shift a nation and bring an exodus out of slavery for many and create a new beginning in their lives. I believe this is true not only for human trafficking victims, but also for Hurting Moms and Grieving Moms. *Me*

The number 5 has still continued to come up over and over since we got back to the United States. I went to a city book festival and signed up for a workshop dealing with some topics in the entertainment industry. While I was sitting in the auditorium, which was on the campus of a well-known university, I looked up at the seat in front of me. Someone had taken chalk and wrote 55 on the seat in front of me. There were no other seats that had writing on it...only the seat where I was sitting.

Just for the record...I work at a college and you do not write on the seats—chalk or anything else! Since we are looking for a producer to make Shari's book into a movie, I felt like it was God's confirmation that indeed this was going to happen, and that we would find favor with the movie.

Back to the Taiwan trip...

"We need to jump on this bus," Cindy exclaimed.

Jet lagged and still getting acclimated to the culture, we rode the bus in silence. I looked out the glazed window and then I saw it. A huge billboard with the words, "For a house call 555-555-5555." My mouth dropped open as I continued to stare at the sign in shock.

Melodie was talking softly into her phone like she did the entire trip, recording what we were seeing; only she saw the other billboard that said, "Buy a house call 888-888-8888." She was recording it on her social media page.

Five was the number we kept getting before we left, and then when we landed in Taiwan we kept getting the number eight. Eight is the number of new beginnings. It is also considered a lucky number in Taiwan—a sign of infinity or Feng Shui.

The number eight continued to show up while we were in the country. When we had gone to our first Airbnb, the owner of this small little apartment we were staying at came by to give us a tour of the place. There was not much to show since it was a small little flat. He showed us all the appliances, heating and air, and water usage rules of the house. As he left he gave us the code to the WIFI. He wrote it down on a scrap of paper and handed it to us…88888888.

It was the number eight…eight times. There it was again. It was a sign, not only of new beginnings, but new beginnings times eight. From the time we landed in the country until the time we left, we all kept seeing the number eight everywhere.

Our plan for this trip was to retrace Shari's steps in her enslavement and go to all the different places she had been held as a slave, and let Melodie see and experience those sites. Through the number eight we felt God was saying, "I will give you a new beginning in those old places of slavery."

At every place we went, we watched Shari experience the feeling that she felt as a slave, but something wonderful happened—she found healing in those places where she was able to release the feelings associated with that place and attach a new meaning; a new meaning of freedom. There was a release that happened. The more places we went, the more she found a new freedom she had never had before. I felt as though I were watching her truly get emotionally free for the very first time. Shari felt safe to find healing because she was surrounded by people who loved and truly cared about her. By us being there it created a type of womb where she could feel safe enough to heal.

Watching Shari at each physical place that represented her enslavement, and then watching her find freedom in those places, was truly something that only God could do. Twenty years of therapy could not do what was done in ten days in Taiwan. Shari begin to live the very title of her book, **My Name Is Also Freedom**!

BACKSTORY

It's been almost a full year since we went to Taiwan and I still get 5's and 8's at different places I go. One time I was right in the middle of making a huge shift in my company and I met a friend for coffee. When I got to the front door of the coffee place I froze and just stared at the window with the name of the place in full view. The name of the coffee house was 1888. It was not the address of the coffee place, but the actual name. Who names their coffee house 1888?! Well this guy did—and boy did I pay attention to that meeting and what we were discussing. Whenever I get that number, I make a mental note about what I am doing and what I am thinking. Usually I get that number when I am worrying about something relating to Shari's book, and it is God's reminder that He's got this book and all of us on the team!

THE PUBLISHER

The day we arrived at Elim Publishing there was a Christian bookstore with a sign that said, 'Jesus Loves You.' Even through that simple message, Shari had a good feeling about this publisher and loved the literal sign we were given. I felt very strongly from my prayer time the night before that God had said Elim was our publisher, so we all went into the meeting filled with hope.

Years earlier I had done some consulting for a commercial developer that was building upscale movie theaters in China. I had several meetings with Chinese businessmen, so it gave me practice learning the culture and proper things to do in a business meeting. One of the big cultural things I learned was when presenting your business card to someone, you face the card towards them cupped in both of your hands with a slight bow to 'present the card.'

I also found out through prior business experience that building the relationship is of utmost importance and that you are not to talk about the business deal until well into the second or third meeting with someone. I had all our team's business cards translated into Mandarin Chinese as well as English. I had done my homework going into this meeting, now it was up to God to do the rest. Little did I know how much God was going to flip this whole meeting around.

As we walked into the back offices at Elim Publishing, we thought we were going to have a meeting with one of the publisher's assistants, but when we got there we were led into the office of the president of the company!

The president of Elim Publishing was a very nice, but serious man, in a full black suit and tie—very formal. His assistant joined us to help in the translation along with Cindy who was our interpreter. Throughout this process, we ended up giving Cindy the official title, Director of Asian Publishing.

The meeting began very formal with all of us bowing and introducing ourselves. Elder James Huang, the president of the company, led off the conversation by asking us some questions about Shari.

"We are a Christian publishing company," he began.

"Most of our books have a strong Christian focus with a lot of Bible teaching. Will Shari's book be similar to that format?" He kicked off the questioning.

"Is Shari a Christian? What is her book about?" He kept firing the questions.

There were a lot of direct questions that I needed to answer as honestly as I could.

At this point, I decided to keep it simple and straightforward with my answers.

"It is her story...plain and simple. It is not going to have a bunch of Scriptures in the book because it is simply her story." I started off.

Well, he was still listening so that was good, I thought to myself.

I told him the story of how I met Shari and how I felt God impress upon my heart that Shari's message mattered and to tell her story. I kept it as simple as I could and hoped that it would be enough to satisfy him.

A year before the trip, I felt God impress upon my heart:

"Shari's book will be like a tsunami (in a good way) and impact a nation."

I wondered on several occasions after that..."Was that God or just me?"

Three days before I left for Taiwan, I had my answer.

I was listening online to a women's conference late at night on my computer and Havilah Cunnington was the speaker. At the end of her message she asked if there was anyone in the room that flew in from Taiwan to the conference. One woman in the very back stood up.

Havilah said she felt that "There was a tsunami of the presence of God…I feel like there is a rescue for girls in that country and the women are getting their voices back."

My mouth dropped open…I am around the prophetic culture quite a bit and I have never heard someone use the word tsunami before in a prophetic word. I was completely floored that out of hundreds of messages I could choose from on the church's website, I 'happened' to select that three-day conference and the exact day of the conference that this word was being given to this Taiwanese woman. Now I knew for sure I had heard God correctly when he spoke to me about what Shari's book would accomplish.

As I began to speak to Elder Huang, those words came flooding back to me. If I had not received that confirmation three days earlier, I am not sure I would have shared it with him. It was a surreal moment as I shared with him what the Lord had spoken to me.

I told him the plain and simple story and then he repeated it right back to me exactly the way I said it. I could tell it was sinking deep into his spirit and that he 'got it'.

At that point, the atmosphere shifted in the room and I felt God's spirit so tangible in his office that you could touch it. I was not expecting what came next.

Elder Huang began to share an experience he had in college when he went to visit a tribal village close to the same area as Shari's township. He said he watched a tribal girl being sold right in front of him. He saw the money and the liquor being exchanged and the young tribal girl started kicking and screaming as they took her away.

"There was nothing I could do. I did not have the money to save her.

...and I've been looking for her ever since that day to save her," he said as tears starting streaming down his face.

All of us began to cry as we realized we were in a very special and holy moment. He then proceeded to tell us that four years earlier he was diagnosed with stage-four cancer and was given only a couple months to live. He said that one of the churches in a tribal village fasted and prayed for him and he was healed.

Not only had this wonderful God-fearing man seen first-hand a tribal girl being sold, but he technically should have been dead and not even here speaking to us at that moment! Not only that, but he got cancer around the same time I met Shari and began working with her on her book.

Wow!

There are simply no words to describe what had taken place. That meeting would have rocked even the strongest person.

We all sat in silence taking in that sacred moment, when Shari said, "I would like to share my story with you."

She then proceeded to share the story of her father selling her when she was seven years old. She explained how her perpetrators moved to the United States and the story of how she got free twenty years later. Tears flowed from Elder Huang's face at the same time tears streamed down all of our faces, as we realized the importance of that meeting and the God-encounter we were having.

Elder Huang said, "I have always wanted to tell the story of a girl from the tribal village."

In this crescendo moment in the meeting, I pointed at him and then pointed at Shari and said, "This is your girl!"

Forty-five wonderful minutes went by in the thickest God-environment I have ever been in when Elder James Huang said, "We would like to publish your story."

I was stunned at first, but then panic sunk in. That is not what the cultural books (that I had read) said he would do. I was not ready for him to say he wanted a deal on the spot.

He continued, "You have these two options."

He explained in detail the two options. Then he asked me which option I wanted. Flashbacks from the flight attendant lady at the counter asking me for the $600 came flooding back to me, but I was not ready to make a decision on the spot.

"I need to pray about it," I stammered.

❧ BACKSTORY ☙

Later when we returned to Taipei after traveling around Taiwan, I had made up my mind which deal we would take with Elim. The option we took came with great faith, knowing God had provided in miraculous ways already on the trip, especially with the airport provision still fresh on my mind.

THE HOUSE OF PRAYER

After our meeting with Elder Huang, we said goodbye with cultural bows as his assistant took us to another room. It was a small sanctuary in a room down the hall. It was set up like an IHOP (International House of Prayer) model where there was a map of the world covering the entire wall. There were gridlines through the map and the members of the church took turns and had been praying in that room for twenty-four hours a day, seven days a week, for four years!

As we walked into that room, simultaneously all of us dropped to our knees and began to cry out to God how unworthy we were and how great He is. It was one of the most holy experiences I have ever felt. It was a 'kiss the carpet'...'God you are amazing'...'I am so unworthy' moment I will never forget. With four years of intercession and praise twenty-four hours a day, the atmosphere was very holy.

There were three beautiful ladies who were in the room praying. They said that most people who come to the prayer room, fall to their knees in the presence of God. As we were worshiping God, I noticed a communion tray by the worship leader. I asked one of the women if we could take communion. She said yes and went to the back room to prepare the bread and grape juice. She came back with fresh elements and we took communion together on the floor in a very reverent atmosphere. I have taken communion in Israel before, but this experience was by far the most holy experience I have ever had. We soaked in His presence for some time and we did not want to leave.

After communion, the women explained how they pray and worship every day. They showed us a map of the world and said that they pray for different parts of the world in two-hour increments according to the grid lines on the map. Right when we walked in they were praying for the United States, and not only the United States, but the part of the United States where we live. I looked at the map where she pointed and there was a star on the map to represent the big city in our local area. When I saw the star representing our area, I realized that they had been praying for our city right when we walked into that prayer room. I completely lost it!

I was so undone by God's presence and perfect timing. There are people in the faith community that talk about being 'undone' or 'wrecked' in the presence of God. I think I now know what they are talking about.

It was the first time in my life when I seriously asked the Lord to stop.

"Stooooop!" I exclaimed.

"I cannot handle any more of you God." I said with a slow cadence.

I have never told God to stop before. I simply could not handle any more of His goodness or His presence in that moment. It is a wild place to be with God.

When we were ready to leave, I explained to the Taiwanese women why we were there and showed them one of the Square Tree Publishing business cards which has a gold logo of a square tree.

One of the ladies said, "Wait right here."

She ran to the back room and came out with a pamphlet.

She said, "Not only were we praying for your city when you walked into the room, but we also pray for the twelve tribes of Judah at certain times of the day. The tribe we were praying for when you walked in was the Tribe of Asher. Asher was the eighth tribe of Judah (which was the number we kept getting when we landed in the country). Asher means 'The Prosperous One.'

She then proceeded to show me the tribal picture of Asher which was the picture of a tree, which she said looked like my company logo. At this point I was completely undone...yet again.

I could not be more undone. Wrecked or undone does not even begin to describe how I felt in that moment.

I am forever changed from this encounter with God. I will never be the same. I pray that this encourages you as well for whatever you are going through. God knows where you are at and what you are going through. God is HUGE! Bigger than we give him credit for at times.

All of the Square Tree team left that day forever changed by simply being in God's true presence. God's pure, raw, unreligious presence where people are willing to give him the space and time to move in big ways, is the most priceless thing we encountered. If this is any indication of what God is about to accomplish with this book, then we stand in great expectation to see what God is about to do!

✥ BACKSTORY ✥

After the meeting at Elim Publishing, Cindy helped Shari pick out the very first Bible Shari ever bought for herself. It was a leather-bound Bible with a double translation in both English and Mandarin. Shari walked out of the bookstore grasping the Bible and holding it tightly to her chest like a long-lost treasure. That night when we all got back to the Airbnb, Cindy sat down with Shari at the kitchen table. Cindy helped Shari read her very first words she has ever read in a Bible and they started in the book of Matthew. There are simply no words that can describe that time, except to say priceless!

THE LUNCH

We ended up traveling all around Taiwan, and we did not hear back from Elim again even though we had sent them an email thanking them for their hospitality and offer. I was beginning to get worried, but I felt God give me peace over the situation. Something just did not seem right after such an amazing meeting and God-encounter that they did not respond. When we arrived back in Taipei at the end of our trip, I suggested to the team that we go back to Elim's bookstore in hopes of running into the president's assistant again.

When we arrived at the bookstore, we asked for the assistant we had come to really like and had an amazing talk with her. She said that they did email us back and we found out later that the email had gotten lost in one of the files on Cindy's computer. We were relieved that they were still interested in publishing Shari's book. We left the bookstore happy that the deal was still on the table.

surrealism – 1920 dreamlike
imagery – capture thoughts
of unconscious mind.
influences, Abstractism

Sherry Ward with Shari Ho

"Hello, this is Simone," Cindy heard on the cell phone.

"Elder Huang would like to take you out to lunch. Are you available?" Simone asked.

"Yes," Cindy said with excitement.

We arranged to meet the following day for our first Dim Sum lunch. It was a nice restaurant and what struck me the most was that Shari's seat was placed right next to the president of the publishing company. It was surreal to see Shari, who was treated as a slave and brainwashed to believe some horrible things about her self-worth, now seated next to the president of a large Taiwan Publishing company. She was being lifted up right before our eyes.

Shari and Elder Huang looked at the menu together and in Mandarin he asked her if there was anything we did not eat. She said we would eat anything, except she asked if they would take the heads off of any meat that was served at our table. Elder Huang seemed to enjoy this comment.

Once the meal came, we were given very nice chop sticks that were slippery. I know how to eat with chop sticks, but the ones I have used in the past were made of wood. These were the real deal, but slippery. The entire meal I was afraid I would fling my food across the table and a waiter would have to catch it!

One of the things I learned in Taiwan is to leave food on your plate. After all those years of my mom telling me to eat

70

everything on my plate because there are starving people in the world, this flew in direct opposition to what I had been taught to do. If you eat all your food in this culture, it is assumed that you want more, so needless to say I was extremely full after that meal and you could have rolled me out of the restaurant.

At the end of the conversation, Elder Huang asked me, "Have you thought about the offers I have given you?"

"Yes," I said wondering if I had to decide on the spot.

"Which offer would you like to take?" He said.

I felt like the *Let's Make A Deal* game show where I had to choose between Box #1 and Curtain #2. Hoping that I had chosen correctly I said, "Option #2." Although this option was the more expensive of the two, I knew it was the right one for each person involved.

I gulped really hard and had a flashback to the airport when the attendant asked me for the $600...only there was a lot more at stake with this decision. God proved himself at the airport, yet this was a new level for which I needed to trust Him.

This was the best option for everyone who had worked on the book, and now it was simply trusting God yet again. There would be a lot of trusting Him on this trip, but oh what a God-adventure it was!

⚜ BACKSTORY ⚜

There is a special video moment between Shari and me that is captured on social media. Click below to check out the moment I told Shari that we would say 'yes' and have Elim publish her book. The look of excitement on Shari's face is priceless!

www.freedomhasaname.com/Elim

THE DARK PLACES

"I'm going to Taiwan," I would tell people before the trip.

"Wow! Why are you going to go on the trip?" they would ask excitedly.

"I'm going with a human traffic survivor to reenact her enslavement," I would say with excitement.

I do not think I used the correct word when I said 'reenact', but I was not sure which word to use to describe what we were going to do. I did not really grasp how that sounded until I got the same response from a few different people.

"Oh…," they would say in a sad manner.

The mood would totally change in the conversation and they would not know what to say after that.

"No, you don't understand," I would say. "This is a trip to give her a new beginning."

Instinctively, I knew that Shari was going to find a new beginning for her life when she faced the difficulties of her past by going to the dark places where she was enslaved. But how do you explain that kind of history with someone only asking me where I am going on vacation this year? They were thinking Hawaii or some other luxurious destination in the world, not a reenactment of a human trafficked girl's story. I decided it was best to leave some things unsaid.

Our first stop was in Taipei, the capital of Taiwan. This was the first place Shari was taken when she was sold, and she lived there for many years. The sights and smells of this exotic place were very different from the rural village where she grew up. Shari took the Square Tree team to many of the places that she went to when she was a slave. Melodie was especially interested in this part of the trip, because she wanted to get the exact feel of the places that Shari went to as a young girl.

One of the common things Shari did when she was young was to go to the day markets with The Old Lady that held her captive. They would walk up and down through the streets buying whatever The Old Lady needed. Vendor after vendor meant bag after heavy bag to carry home. Shari would be forced to carry all of them. The Old Lady had a hard time walking and really needed a cane, but was too prideful to carry one at times, so Shari became her human cane. The Old Lady insisted on using Shari's shoulder to lean her full weight upon as she walked. Even now, Shari has back and neck issues because of this and has a hard time when people touch her shoulders.

Shari's first step in her healing process on our Taiwan trip came in this day market. In the past she was forced to shop, cook, and clean for The Old Lady. But on this trip, the trip when she was free, she chose to prepare dinner for us because she wanted to, not because anyone was forcing her to cook for us. So off she went to the market with Melodie in tow to buy all the ingredients she needed for a typical Taiwanese meal to prepare for us.

There was only one rule that Melodie gave her—she was not to carry any of the food that they purchased. Melodie wanted to carry all the bags so that she could walk in Shari's footsteps when she was a slave, and feel what it was like to carry all those heavy bags. Shari insisted on paying for the meal herself even though she did not have a lot of money on the trip. Melodie let her pay and Shari was so proud of being able to spend her own money.

This time going to the day market was fun for Shari, and it was one of the places on her list she wanted to go when we arrived in Taipei. She had an amazing time at the market picking out the vegetables and fish that she was going to prepare for us. She had money in her pocket and she was able to buy some of her favorite dishes from the food vendors on the street. One of Shari's favorite 'snacks' is chicken feet and chicken heart on a stick. She gobbled it up and wanted more!

They both came back to the flat, and Shari prepared a traditional fish dinner that was amazing to the senses! This trip to the market, as simple as it seems, was a very profound trip and one example of how God was turning around the bad memories and replacing them with brand new good memories. Not only did Shari get to hand select everything she wanted for the meal, she was also able to pay for it with her own money and prepare it for those that she cared about, and not because she was forced. It was the first step in the 'number eight new beginnings' healing that was taking place on this trip.

Another common place The Old Lady took Shari was to this stunningly beautiful park. The Old Lady loved to walk every day for exercise, come rain or shine, which in Taipei means a lot of rainy days. The Old Lady was very vain about her appearance and meticulous about her health, so this was a daily ritual for both of them. When we were in Taipei, we hopped on a local bus that took us about forty-five minutes to get to the same park that Shari went to with The Old Lady most days. Some of Shari's memories are fuzzy, so we had to navigate her recollections to find just the right park. When we got to the park, it was filled with beautiful foliage of aged trees and winding stairways going over streams. It was very peaceful and serene. I could not imagine anything but peaceful feelings about this serene park, but it was not for Shari when she was young.

Shari took us to this special place in the park with an older tree that had been cut into the shape of a box at the top. It was her favorite tree in the entire park.

Serene ~ other calm unruffled repose Quietude

76

"Hello Mr. Tree," Shari began.

"Do you remember me?" She said.

"I used to come here and see you when I was little. When I came here I was a slave, but I wanted to let you know, Mr. Tree, that I am free now!" She exclaimed with true happiness, as tears flowed down my face as I watched, standing behind her.

I do not know if Shari literally hugged that tree, but every part of her being did!

She stayed a long while with that tree, enjoying the park like others had for years, but now with a new-found freedom for the very first time. This was a redemptive moment in Shari's journey on this trip with many more new beginnings in store.

The sacredness of that moment has been forever etched in all on our hearts and minds.

Shari's story is a story of redemption. That was the purpose of the trip...to bring about new memories. New beginnings to a past that needed redeeming.

As we stood looking at that special tree, I was struck by the fact that the top of the tree had been cut into a huge square. I looked up and saw the square cut out of the tree and then it dawned on me—the name of my company is *Square Tree Publishing*! Fresh tears began to run down my face as I sensed

God's providential hand in both of our lives coming together in this sacred moment.

It was an honor and a privilege to walk through many other parts of town with Shari. Each place that we visited, Shari was able to replace old bad memories, with fresh new happy memories with trusted friends. The old bad memories were quickly being replaced by new ones with people she cared about and whom she loved. It was a safe place. It was a new place. It was a new beginning for her.

One of the toughest places that we visited was walking down the street where she was held captive in an apartment flat. We walked that street at night as a soft, drizzling rain lightly hit our umbrellas, like the tears that had been shed in that place. It was such a dark night, it echoed the sentiments that Shari had for this place. We each walked silently down that somber dark street while taking in the buildings below and apartments above. We stopped for what seemed like an eternity at the exact place where she was held prisoner all those years.

Quietly we walked with the tapping sound of the rain, as Shari recounted story after story of what took place in that apartment flat. Stories of a little girl looking out the window seeing other kids going off to school, wishing for the day that she could sport a backpack full of school supplies and go with them. But she was never allowed to go to school. Or the daily ritual of walking up the hill to a local church with The Old Lady leaning on her shoulder. Stories of The Old Lady beating and kicking her at the least perceived offense. None of us dared to speak, for we wanted to feel the full weight of what this little girl had gone through. That street in Taipei is relatively unchanged, but we are not the same—forever changed by the visual picture of Shari's imprisonment.

We were not sure how God was going to redeem this part of her journey, but after a half hour we continued walking to the end of the street where there was a local restaurant well off the beaten tourist track, and we ordered our usual beef soup with noodles. We talked and laughed as we sat on hard chairs at a rickety old table. We had a great time eating just steps away from the very place she was held captive. Laughter is great medicine, and somehow, Shari began to find healing from the experience by confronting her past head on.

✑ BACKSTORY ✑

The experience of walking down the street where she was held captive was the weightiest location of the entire trip. The rain echoed the sentiments that night, and the whole atmosphere of the place helped us to feel what Shari must have felt when she was a slave. In order to heal, we need to face some of the tough places of our past to then move on with trusted loved ones and friends to find the hope and healing we need. I'm not sure how, other than through God, but that is what Shari was able to do that night!

THE HILLSIDE CHURCH

The weekly trek with The Old Lady up the hill to the local church each Sunday was one of Shari's reprieve days, if only for just a couple of hours. When she was sitting in church, The Old Lady had to be on her best behavior in front of the pastor and the members of the church. It was the only place where The Old Lady did not yell at her or hit her. Shari would often fall asleep in the pews, collapsed from the sheer exhaustion of the week.

The night we walked the street where she was held captive and had ducked into a local restaurant, Shari began to recount her memories being in that hillside church. The church was a peaceful place and somehow, even though many times she fell asleep, she found God there. The members of the church were very nice to her as The Old Lady would always call Shari her 'granddaughter.' Although there may have been suspicions that Shari was not her granddaughter, no one ever said anything to Shari. She could tell that some of the members felt sorry for her and gave her gifts as a way to make it better. Later, however, The Old Lady would yell at her and many times take them away. There was an undeniable peace that permeated that church. Although The Old Lady was abusive and supposedly a Christian, it did not stop Shari from finding God. She would hear His still, small voice in the smallest of ways, and as she began to recount those memories it was a magical moment in the rain in the small, locals-only restaurant.

 BACKSTORY

It still amazes me today that Shari found God in the midst of being with an abusive perpetrator that had a Bible in one hand and was beating her with the other hand. It is a miracle that she found the true God of the Bible in the middle of such incongruity. God was still able to speak to her despite the HUGE contradiction of the situation. Shari still follows that still small voice that has led her all these years.

THE MUSEUM

On the far side of Taipei, we walked the streets where Shari would come with The Old Lady to buy these special mushrooms and herbs. Every weekend they would take a long bus ride to this part of the city, but this day, with the people who cared about her, she had an entirely new reason for coming.

We stopped in to visit one of the organizations called the Taipei Women's Rescue Foundation. Shari was familiar with this organization because they help women who were human trafficked. The last time Shari was here they had three different aftercare program locations for the young women. We learned a very big cultural lesson that day. In Taiwan, you just do not drop in on someone; you need to come announced and with an appointment, but they were very gracious and invited us into their offices anyway. We were able to meet the program director and also the president of the organization. They gave us material and talked about the different issues their organization was involved in and the programs they offer. We were sad to hear that the three different aftercare locations for the trafficked girls had now become only one location due to lack of funding. Their new focus was on women of domestic abuse and they have places and programs to give these victims hope. We told them that next time we come, Shari would like to visit the human trafficked girls at the last location they have open.

We also found out that this organization has a beautiful new museum called the Ama Museum, which means 'grandmother' in Mandarin. They invited us the next day to come for a private tour. The architecture was stunning and so well thought out; it had won several prestigious design awards. The top floor was dedicated to the 'comfort women' of WWII who were lured with promises of work in factories or an education for a better life by the Japanese army, but instead they were made prisoners, forced to sleep with multiple soldiers in caves on the front lines at night. The bottom floor of the museum was dedicated to the survivors of human trafficking. They asked Shari if they could film her story and put her video and book in their museum. They also wanted Shari to encourage other people to come to their museum, so they filmed her inviting people to this beautiful place. Shari was a bit nervous at first, but then once she began filming, she did amazing!

One of the hallways in this museum was extremely unique and very creatively designed. It had long cylinder tubes hanging down with a light inside each one. As we put our hand under the light of the clear tube there was a name of one of the women who had been trafficked. Some of the tubes were clear and some were made of bronze. The tubes made of bronze had lights inside similar to the clear ones, except that they did not have any names. We were confused at first why some of the tubes had names under the light and why some of them did not. Our museum guide said the ones with no names represented the women that were yet to be found in human trafficking.

It was one of the most moving design features I have ever seen. The designer had placed the Scripture from Isaiah 42:3-4b on a bronze piece of metal on the wall that says...

*"A bruised reed he will not break, and a
smoldering wick he will not snuff out. In
faithfulness he will bring forth justice; he will
not falter or be discouraged till he establishes
justice on earth."*

I stood there staring at this part of the museum letting the weightiness of this design feature have its full impact. The museum carried the same heaviness of a holocaust museum that I had been to, and it made a deep and abiding impact on me that day.

The Ama Museum bookstore had items that were made by the survivors, and we each purchased a specially made item to support their museum. As we wrapped up our private tour of the museum, they gave us a thick picture book with the women's stories along with how the museum was designed.

At the end of the tour, they thanked Shari for sharing her story on film. Then they invited Shari to come back and have a book signing at their museum when her book came out. We were all floored yet again. God was moving in ways we did not see coming!

In the U.S. publishing world this is not normally the way it works. Usually a book is released in the United States—it does well—then you get an international foreign rights deal, and then you get book signings. I love how God turned this upside down and how we were offered a book signing venue BEFORE the book even came out, and BEFORE we got an international foreign rights deal! God was showing us from the very start that this is not an ordinary book and that the *traditional* ways of doing things is not what He has in mind for Shari's story. We are truly blessed to have made new friends at this museum. It was one of the most stunning museums I have ever seen, and I am looking forward to coming back for Shari's book signing there.

❧ BACKSTORY ❧

I am still amazed that when we planned the trip we had 'no agenda', yet God opened so many doors and had a far greater agenda then we could have ever had. One of my close friends was praying for me while I was on the trip and she felt God tell her, "Pray for Sherry, she has no plans in Taiwan." She began arguing with God…"What do you mean she has no plans…Sherry always has a plan." Little did she know that we truly went to a foreign country with no agenda and relatively no plans—yet it was the best God-adventure I have been on so far. That day we secured a book signing location before Shari's book has even come out yet.

THE ALISHAN MOUNTAIN

Shari wanted to go to a famous mountain called Alishan. Many people from all over the country go to this mountain to specifically see the sunrise. When it came time to go to Alishan Mountain, we were carrying all this luggage for a one-day trip there. We felt bad because even the bus driver struggled to get our luggage out of the bottom of his bus, and we think he threw out his back carrying our luggage. A day later when it came time for the driver to pick us up, he was nowhere to be found and they used a different driver!

Shari is the second of six sisters. Her baby sister, whom we named Charlie, and her adopted parents were able to come and meet us at Alishan. Shari had not seen her sister in years, so it was a tear-filled reunion. Shari was able to stay with them through the night catching up and reconnecting to her family. It was a healing time to reunite with her baby sister whom she loved and tried to protect fiercely while growing up.

The next morning we had to get up at 3:00 a.m. to begin our trek up the mountain. We ended up buying some gloves and hand warmers because it was freezing cold...literally we saw a temperature sign that said it was 0 degrees Celsius. After we trekked up a hill, we got to an old railway train that looked like the one at our local amusement park. It was open on all sides, and the cold air hit our face as we braved the forty-five-minute journey to the top, with Shari's sister Charlie and her friends in tow.

Once we got to the top of the mountain, there was an extremely funny Taiwanese guy telling jokes and making everyone laugh. Even though Melodie and I did not know what he was saying, you could tell he was a funny guy with his flailing arms and funny voice. He sounded like he was selling stuff, like a carnival barker. I found out that humor transcends any language barrier. He was filling the time until the sun broke through the clouds for the sunrise.

That particular day was perfectly timed. It had been raining for the past two weeks, and the morning we went happened to be the first day the sun came out! It was so symbolic of our trip and Shari's life, like so many of the things we witnessed being on the trip. When the sun came peeking through the clouds, there was a hushed silence in the huge crowd at the top of the mountain. It was a very special moment to watch the sun come up. It was very symbolic of new beginnings, which was the theme of the trip once we landed in Taiwan. This mountainside sunrise was just the beginning of a new season in Shari's life, and we had front row seats on this new adventure.

After we saw the sunrise, we hiked back down the mountain. It reminded me of Yosemite National Park in the United States. Steams, ponds, and waterfalls in a lush green background of trees and bridges covered the pathway as we leisurely walked back to the hotel. Alishan Mountain is a beautiful place and will hold a special memory for our team.

BACKSTORY

We filmed the book trailer on this beautiful mountain. In the book trailer, there are parts where Shari is on a bridge looking around and walking in a beautiful green forest area. This is the Alishan forest and mountain, where we saw the sun rise.

THE DAWU TOWNSHIP

Dawu Township was the place where Shari was born and where the majority of her family still lives today. We took a bumpy bus trip and then a long train ride to get there, once again toting all our luggage, but it was worth the trip. It was a beautiful township on the southeastern shore of Taiwan. Her sisters and brothers picked us up in the middle of the night, and it was the first glimpse we had of Shari's town.

In the morning, we went with her siblings and took a ride along the coast. It is stunningly beautiful, with the coastline beaches on one side, and the hilltops where Shari used to live on the other side. We went to the second house that Shari's parents lived in after she was sold. The house sat on a hilltop overlooking the water with a grass field above it. It was a mixture of aluminum siding and concrete and a host of other material patched together to make a house.

This home was similar to the house that Shari lived in when she was little. We stood outside as we debated whether we were going to knock on the door so that we could see inside, but chose not to bother the new tenants of the house. We were content enough to just see the outside and walk along the path leading up to her house from long ago.

Shari's family is so large and most of the names Melodie and I had trouble pronouncing, so I decided to give Shari's family American nicknames. We tried to match their name to a common American name that sounded the most like their original name. We named her sisters in order; Susan, Ingrid, Charlene, Yoli, and Charlie. Shari's step-brothers are Chan, Gary, Sony, and step-sister Sonia. Throughout the trip we kept forgetting which name we gave to which family member and we had many laughs trying to figure out which name was which! Once we got the names down it was much easier to reference them in a story. Shari's family history is varied. She has a blended family, so getting the names straight was the first thing that helped us figure out each part to her story as we traveled with her.

One of Shari's greatest desires was to see her mom in her hometown. Circumstances prevented her from seeing her the time before, so we were all praying Shari would be able to see her mom this time. She has forgiven her mom and would truly like a relationship with her.

Through some tough circumstances, Shari was able to see her mom for only five minutes. Even though the visit was cut short, Shari was extremely grateful for the few moments she got with her mom.

After we met with her mom, we had a big BBQ at Charlene's house to meet her family and other close friends that have been instrumental in helping Shari integrate back into her tribe. The BBQ smells that are typical in America with pork and beef rose in the air, but with a different flair of foods that were completely new to us, including Shari's favorite food…gingerwine soup with chicken feet. Of course, there was also fried fish with their heads intact staring at us as we ate them!

What struck me the most about the Dawu township is their hospitality. The BBQ was truly a feast that went on for hours and into the middle of the night. More and more food kept coming as the night progressed. They truly know how to enjoy each other's company and not be rushed to get on to their next activity like we too often do in America.

We finally said our goodbyes at 8:00 p.m. and the BBQ was still going strong. Shari stayed behind for some sister bonding and spent the night to catch up on a world of stories from each of their lives.

 BACKSTORY

Charlene made this special soup they called 'lucky soup.' It was small multi-colored rice balls in a broth. It looked really good, but I did not realize is was full of sugar and very sweet. I tried my best to gulp it down to be polite, after all it was their lucky soup, but after taking one bite I could not swallow as much as I tried. I casually went to the bathroom to spit it out in the trash can. Too late…Melodie said loud enough so that everyone could hear, "Were you spitting out that soup?" I was caught!

THE VILLAGE GIRLS

Shari was the smallest of all her other sisters. Because she was so small, she was not big enough to be sold into the factories, so that it why she was peddled to a woman to be labored trafficked. The original contract for her indentured servitude was for a set amount of time, but years later when her sisters returned to bring her back home, The Old Lady had filled her with fears of being resold, so she stayed. When Shari first went to her captor's house, The Old Lady complained to Shari's father that she was too small and unable to do the work she needed around the house, and reminded her every day of her shortcomings mercilessly. Shari was not alone in being sold.

Dawu Township is integral to Shari's heritage and her story is not uncommon among the tribal girls many decades ago. As we visited the village, we were told of other stories of girls sold to the factories and locked in cages at night suffering horrible working conditions. With little counseling offered in the village to get help, I would venture to guess that the memories of the past have probably haunted many of the now grown women in the tribe.

While we were in her township, Shari wanted to go to one of the local churches in the village. On Sunday morning we all put on our best clothes and walked down to the local church. It reminded me of some of the smaller churches that I ministered to as a high schooler on mission's trips. It had a familiar balcony where the kids hung out during worship with their sandaled feet dangling from the railing from the second floor. They sang some songs that I thought I recognized, only they were in another language. The sweet music was very uplifting and continued as we watched a woman pastor clothed in a robe come up to preach.

We watched the pastor preach with enthusiasm with her hands, telling the story. Melodie and I did not understand anything she said, but she seemed very passionate about her message. Then, without notice, the pastor motioned to us to come down and speak to the congregation. I was not expecting this, but we dutifully went down the creaky old winding staircase and stood before the congregation.

The pastor gave Shari the microphone. She wanted Shari and me to give our testimony about Shari's story and writing her book. Shari began to tell her story of being sold, which was a far too common story that many of the congregation already knew about or had experienced themselves. Shari spoke with such conviction and authority I had never seen in her before. I was completely amazed at what she said and the love that she had for these people in her tribe—a tribe she hardly knew because she had left when she was so young.

When Shari was done, they passed the microphone to me. I grasped it with my sweat-filled hands not sure of what I was going to say. I let them know how much we cared about Shari and her township. I shared that our heart for writing Shari's story was not to point fingers at anyone, because the greatest freedom we can have is in forgiveness. The most important part is the redemptive nature of Shari's story.

Many of the congregation seemed to be interested in what Shari and I said, but there were the older ones who were trying to simply stay awake. What struck me the most was that Shari told her story in Taiwan for the very first time without the cameras or the media—editing what she said. Just a raw uncut story of betrayal, loss, and redemption while finding her way back to freedom, her township, and God. The pastor asked if we could come back after Shari's book was done and we agreed. We greeted people outside after the service. Melodie and I mostly smiled and bowed a lot as Shari and Cindy greeted the church members in their native tongue.

Before we had left for our trip, a friend had suggested that I bring gifts to all the people we visited in Taiwan. It was right after Christmas, so I was able to get a lot of chocolate type gifts at my local gift store and bundle them into cute gifts, both big and small, for everyone we met. This was the reason why I ended up with so much luggage. Half of it was filled with chocolate that I hoped would not melt on our long journey. The chocolate did not melt, but the boxes may have a gotten squished along the way.

After the church service, we went into a side room where a bunch of young children asked us a lot of questions. Luckily, I had taken some of the chocolate out of my suitcase to pass out to the children. One of the main reasons Shari wanted to go to church was to see the children. As I looked around the room, I saw one girl who was around seven years old, and I tried not to stare at her. Tears welled up in my eyes as I looked at this young girl, picturing Shari at the same age being sold into captivity.

Today these girls have a chance and an education thanks in part to the Taiwan government who have subsidized many improvements in the township. I was thankful because these girls did not have to be sold. I watched in awe as Shari was stepping into her new leadership role. Her transformation was happening right in front of us—a far cry from even four years earlier when I met her at my local church.

When I met Shari, she had come a long way since being freed—yet she still desperately needed to find healing from being enslaved for twenty years. I watched as she transformed like a beautiful butterfly out of a yoked cocoon into a lovely example of leadership to these young children and especially the young girls. The chocolate helped of course, and many of the kids were asking questions all about America. One girl in particular captured Melodie's heart because she played drums. Melodie had been a worship leader in her church for years playing both drums and bass guitar.

It struck me how different this young girl's life would be compared to Shari's because the township is not destitute like it was years ago. Putting a face to a young girl close to the age that Shari was when she was taken was too much for me. Tears ran down my face yet again. We gave this young girl extra chocolate!

As we went to leave, all the children came around us, giving us big hugs. We were torn because we did not want to leave the kids, but at the same time I realized it was different for these children, they would be safe, unlike Shari.

BACKSTORY

Now that Shari is free, she wants to find ways to give back to her township and these amazing young girls. We have been coming up with different ideas in which we can help her tribe and at the same time give opportunities to these young girls.

SECTION III

BACK HOME

*"The Spirit of the Sovereign Lord is on me,
because the Lord has anointed me…
He has sent me to bind up the brokenhearted, to
proclaim freedom for the captives
and release from darkness for the prisoners."*

—Isaiah 61:1

Shari's favorite - Chicken heart and feet!

BBQ at Shari's sister's house

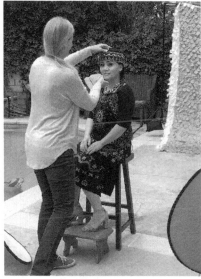

Grilled fish looking at us!

Photo shoot day!

Shari with her author Melodie

Shari with Elder Huang

Shari's speech teacher Brenda

Taiwan team

THE COUPLE

When Shari found her freedom, there was a special couple that 'adopted' her in the United States and took it upon themselves to take care of her and help her the best they could. They wanted to write about Shari, so this is their story in their own words.

"I vividly remember the day I met Shari. The Salvation Army staff contacted me through a church sister, hoping that I could help a Taiwanese girl who was a survivor of human trafficking. I had many doubts in my mind. Maybe they made a mistake on where she was from.

"Taiwan? How can such a horrific thing happen in such an affluent place? I found it hard to believe. I went home to talk to my husband that night, and we both guessed that Shari may have belonged to the 'indigenous people' of Taiwan.

"The next day we met Shari, and we ended up being right that Shari came from a Taiwanese indigenous group. Although Taiwan was economically rich in that era, some indigenous people in the mountains still lived in poor conditions with little property. At that time, it was common for the people of the aborigines to be discriminated against and rejected by society. So many simply gave up their lives, and got involved in gambling and alcoholism, causing many broken families. Children are often the biggest victims of domestic violence and were sold. Shari was one of these victims and was sold by her father when she was seven years old.

"When my husband and I started caring for Shari, we would take her to the restaurant to eat, have dinner with friends, go out and have fun, and occasionally she would come to our house for the night. We treated her as one of our own children.

"Slowly I found out that she had a toughness about her that was not common in a young girl her age. What impressed me the most was that she did not hate her parents. I remember she told me that originally her parents were planning on selling her baby sister, but she took her sister and hid her and asked her parents to sell her first and not her baby sister.

"Shari has had a kind heart even from an early age and understands things that are far beyond her age. Even though The Old Lady who bought her beat her and deprived her of all her freedom and the right to read and write, Shari did not hate her. Shari often told me about her previous life, which was actually very distressing. Her toughness and brave personality are particularly admirable. She is not afraid of environmental difficulties.

"Although she never attended school, she learned to speak fluent English with an American accent in two years. She is very smart, not afraid of challenges, and she even got a job. Her eagerness, hard work ethic, and beautiful life qualities and character made me truly admire her from the bottom of my heart.

"Shari is a person who will remember someone else and give them a gift, even if it is a small thing—she will remember. She often mentions some small things that me or my husband have done for her and she ALWAYS remembers. She is a very grateful person. Her current job requires her giving a lot of love to children, and she is very caring.

"Shari is strong, intelligent, open-minded, caring, forgiving, grateful, hardworking, and a fearless person. With so many years of care and friendship, Shari is like one of our own children. When my husband and I decided to leave the United States and go overseas as missionaries, the only thing I worried about was Shari. But thank God that He raised up a group of brothers and sisters in the church to care for her, accompany her, and to help her.

"Now that she has lived independently and has her own career, we can fulfill the call and mission of God in our life without worrying about her because we know she is well-cared for. This will help us to reach more people overseas and bless more people.

"Praise the Lord. God is the Lord who cares for the orphans!"

Written by Lou and Jenna

"Father of orphans, champion of widows,
is God in his holy house.
God makes homes for the homeless,
leads prisoners to freedom."

—Psalm 68:5-6a (MSG)

 **BACKSTORY**

Cindy, who was the interpreter that went with us to Taiwan, was the woman who this couple mentioned as taking care of Shari and watching over her when they left to be missionaries overseas. Cindy has a small Bible study group, and everyone in that group rallied around Shari after this wonderful couple left. They still support Shari to this day to help her with things that she needs.

THE MISSIONARY

I went to a writer's conference in my local area, and they had a special VIP dinner that I attended. It was cozy with a warm fire going in the fireplace, even though our winters are not very cold. I met a couple of ladies at the event and found out that one of them was a missionary in Taiwan in the 1980s, when she was in her early 20s. At the time there were very few Christians in the country.

I explained why we went to Taiwan and she began to ask me so many questions with such vigor that I was trying to keep up with them all. She wanted to know exact streets names that we had walked, where we stayed, and where we traveled. She was intense in her questioning because decades earlier she had walked those same streets praying for the salvation of the Taiwanese people.

"I tried to commit suicide while I was there," she said almost matter-of-fact.

"Wow!" I said. "What happened?"

She talked about how depressed she had gotten and just wanted to end her life, even though she was a mother of a young child.

She continued the story…

"The day I tried to kill myself I started to walk into the middle of the street because there are so many cars and scooters in that city and I knew that I would be struck and killed," she said.

"Just as I began to step into the middle of the street, one of my friends called me on the phone which startled me, and I remained on the sidewalk talking the call," she continued.

"My friend talked me out of committing suicide that day," she said, relieved to have shared this with me.

The young missionary was not fully recovered from her suicide attempt, but the very next day she went dutifully knocking on doors wanting to share Jesus with the people of Taiwan. Most of the time the people in the apartment flats would not open their door, but this day was different.

"I've been waiting for you," the lady inside the apartment said, as she knocked on the door.

Confused, the missionary asked her what she meant. The lady began to tell her that she had been trying to commit suicide by slicing her wrists and arms with glass that morning.

Her husband came from a different sect in the same religion, which in their culture was forbidden. The lady in the apartment was told by her husband that she was a curse to him because she had given birth to a daughter and not a son. She let her husband's words pierce her heart.

"That is why I want to commit suicide," the lady in the apartment said.

The missionary went on to explain how she shared with this woman God's love for her and that she was not cursed but deeply loved. The lady found God that day and became a Christian.

Tears streamed down my face as my new missionary friend told me this story that happened over forty years ago. What struck me as she was telling me her story is that Shari had tried to commit suicide as well—once by walking into the middle of the street and a friend called her on the phone and saved her from doing it!

God is truly in the business of redeeming situations. The missionary felt God impress upon her that she had a choice. She could end her life if she wanted to, but what He really wanted for her was to help others here on earth, but ultimately the decision was hers to make. She chose life. She chose to serve God. She chose to stay here on earth. It was the same decision that Shari had chosen as well! The parallel was uncanny.

What are the odds that I would meet someone with a story that mirrored Shari's story? This young missionary walked those same streets forty years earlier praying for the people of Taiwan and earnestly wanting them to come to know God. There are no coincidences in God's Kingdom; only divine appointments. This was definitely a divine appointment meeting her.

 BACKSTORY

The whole time I was talking to the missionary, I had this sense that the baton had been given to me to continue running the race that the missionary started. There was a weightiness of responsibility of what this missionary carried and was now being handed off to me. I wanted to run the leg of the race that I had been given well. We held each other in a hug for a very long time, taking in the air of that holy moment.

THE COLLEGE

As we traveled as a team in Taiwan, we watched Shari change right before our eyes. This once sullen, quiet, sad girl was now stepping up into the leadership role to which God had called her. She daily grew into this leadership role while we were in Taiwan.

"I want to help these girls and be a role model for them," Shari told the director of the Taipei Women's Rescue Foundation, an organization that helps human trafficking and domestic violence victims, when we met with them in Taiwan.

As we traveled around Taipei we had to take airplanes, buses, and subways. One day we went down the stairs to the subway station.

"Do you see those words on that sign, Melodie?" Shari asked as we were approaching the underground subway.

"Yes, but I can't read them," Melodie said.

"That is exactly how I feel every day," Shari lamented.

We were beginning to sense and feel what it is like being in a world where you have a hard time reading the signs and the stress of navigating through life with these limitations.

The entire Taiwan trip, especially the kiosks incident at the airport, was a catalyst for Shari to make a change in her life. She realized the importance literacy played, especially now that she was stepping more into a leadership role with speaking engagements.

When Shari was held as a slave, there were many days she looked out the window at the other kids going off to school. She had asked The Old Lady if she could go to school, too, but that was only met with more abuse and chores she had to perform around the house. The Old Lady's sister had looked after Shari several times when she was younger and felt sorry that Shari could not go to school like the other children. She began to teach Shari some Mandarin, but when The Old Lady found out, she exploded in anger to the point of refusing to talk to her sister for years and forbidding her sister to see Shari again.

After returning from Taiwan, Shari was now more determined more than ever to continue her studies. Shari had always wanted to go to college and had attempted several times, but to no avail. Without good reading skills it was extremely hard to navigate the college world.

The first week we were back in the U.S., I took Shari to a local community college. Because I am a part-time professor

116

at a college, I thought helping her would be simple. I thought it would be easy to navigate the counseling office, the testing center, and registration office as a new student at a college. Little did I realize how challenging that task was going to be to get Shari help because of the new confidentiality law called the Family Educational Rights and Privacy Act (FERPA). No one would talk to me because they were not allowed to by law. Shari worked during the day, so we were relegated to navigating the campuses at night when most of the offices were closed. Even when special attempts were made to open an office later than normal, it was such a huge ordeal that it took weeks to get her into an ESL type course. *English Second Language*

Finally, after a month of walking the gauntlet of paperwork, Shari was officially enrolled in an English language class.

We met with the instructor a few weeks before she started class and Shari told the instructor, "I have always wanted to go to school my entire life!"

I was by her side with tears glistening in my eyes.

The instructor said, "I hear that a lot from students that are in my class."

For a moment I was jealous and wanted students in my own college class to have that same drive and motivation.

I went with Shari the first day of class to help her get settled and get her books. Even something as simple as getting books was not easy.

"Use this permission slip to buy your books," the instructor said.

But when we tried, we found out she needed a student ID card, too. Shari could not get the ID card because this was only open for the daytime students! So the futile cycle continued of trying to get everything she needed for this college class.

"Can I help you?" The instructor sneered at me while I was sitting off to the side in the room with Shari.

"I'm here to make sure she is okay and help her get her books," I answered as calmly as I could.

"Well, no one told me...," she replied and began to lay into me.

"...and besides...you are on your phone the whole time. You need to leave," she demanded.

It was true. I was on my phone. I was trying to buy Shari's books on the internet since it was nearly impossible to buy them at the college, even with a permission slip. Ridiculous! I knew this was not a fight I wanted to take on in the classroom, so I politely stepped out in the chilly winter air and sat on the steps outside the classroom for an hour waiting for Shari's class to end.

Shari was very sick during this time and had to take a break outside the classroom because of her extreme coughing episodes. The instructor did not like this very much and used her own words against her and said, "I thought you said you wanted to be in my class so much, and yet you are walking outside."

It did not get much better talking to a specialty counselor. I had to sign a form that allowed me to talk to the counselor with Shari by my side. The first night we walked into the counselor's office, she only let Shari go into the room. Shari insisted that I join them, and that is when the counselor allowed me to go into the room. I was instructed that she did not want me to talk, and that she would be addressing Shari the whole time. She offered Shari some amazing services at the college, but again all of the services were for their daytime students. The counselor suggested that we go to another office on the campus to get some more services, but then said...

"You may not want to tell them that you were human trafficked."

"What?" I thought to myself.

What part of 'she is writing a book and speaking about human trafficking' did the counselor not understand? It was completely beyond my comprehension. She was clearly uncomfortable with the topic and she was a counselor!

A few weeks later that same counselor was shopping in a store and saw Shari. She pretended that she did not see her. That was the last straw for me at that college. We were definitely trying to put a square peg in a round hole.

I then began to pray what I have since dubbed the, 'The Rebecca prayer'. There is a story in the Bible about a man named Abraham who was looking for a wife (companion) for his son Isaac. He sent his worker to find someone for him. His worker went to a neighboring village and looked for the perfect wife (companion) for him.

I began to pray this 'Rebecca prayer' for Shari.

"God help me to find the perfect companion for Shari to find the help she needs to improve her English." Then the thought came to me...Kumon.

From my previous educational background, I knew of Kumon, which is an individualized math and reading program that has a stellar reputation for helping students learn how to read and write. I had seen great results from my students throughout the years. The only thing is that Kumon is usually for younger children.

I called a local Kumon center to find out more information and found a wonderful manager. He was nice and kind and seemed to genuinely care. Shari, Cindy, and I had a meeting with the manager to talk about their services.

He gave us the overview of how they help students learn how to read and write. They gave Shari a test to see at what level of reading she would be starting. With their system, there is one instructor to two students, so technically, Shari would be learning next to a child who was learning his reading. The manager did not want Shari to feel uncomfortable, so he offered to have Shari by herself with one instructor. It was a match made in Heaven. Kumon was the 'Rebecca' we were looking for!

Shari has a one-on-one instructor for Kumon, but one day they were short on instructors, so they sat her next to a three-year-old as they went through the lesson. One of Shari's favorite teachers has a thick Indian accent, and it was a bit challenging to hear the English words pronounced the correct way.

"I don't get it," the little boy said to the instructor.

"Me, either," said Shari.

"I am tired," the little boy moaned again.

"Me too," Shari said as she laughed.

The little boy expressed exactly how Shari felt at times. I do not think he liked doing homework either!

Shari is very thankful for the opportunities that Kumon has given her, and especially grateful that the manager has gone out of his way to help her.

 BACKSTORY

Shari is thriving in this new school setting. She has passed many of the different levels of Kumon and is beginning to grasp the English language better. She is well on her way to becoming proficient in reading and writing. She loves being there, although she does not always like the homework!

THE HEAD DRESS

When Shari was featured on the CNN Freedom Report, the Taiwanese government found out about Shari and right away they began searching the country looking for Shari's family so that they could reunite them again. The Taiwanese government was amazing as they graciously found Shari's real family and paid for her to go back to Taiwan and meet them.

The first time she went back to Taiwan to meet her family, Shari was flanked with numerous bodyguards. The media firestorm was in full force as they followed her everywhere she went in Taiwan, even to the grave site where her father was buried.

Her father had passed away long ago, but her mother, sisters, and brothers were still alive. As she met her mother for the very first time since she had been sold, she hugged her for a very long time. Tears ran down her face as the anger was replaced with forgiveness and all Shari wanted was to see her mother and sisters again. Her mother gave her a beautiful tribal costume that she had sewed for her that she still treasures to this day. There are so many times that Shari's life parallels the story of Joseph in the Bible. This was yet another example because she was given this beautiful costume—this 'coat of many colors.'

When she found out that her mother made her costume, it held an even deeper meaning for her. She had determined to wear it for her photo shoot for the cover of her book. The only thing missing from her costume was the matching head dress.

As we discussed the cover, we wanted Shari to wear her costume as a representation of all the girls that were sold in her village over thirty years ago. Many of these young gals are still there suffering the scares of their enslavement—both physical and emotional. This cover was not just about Shari's story, but it was to represent the story of all of those girls that are still in bondage, either physically or emotionally from the past.

"But what were we going to do without a head dress?" I thought to myself.

We began looking online for a head dress, but we needed one that matched her exact costume that her mother had made her. We found one, but it was very expensive. Then we found another one made by a local village artisan. This seemed to be in alignment with what we wanted to do in representing the village girls. We were on a short timeline because the photo shoot was fast approaching. These were handmade so we were not sure we would get the head dress in time, but what should have taken months only took days.

We found out that this local artisan had just got done making some head dresses for some local girls in the village for a performance they were going to do. It was fitting that this head dress came from one of the village girls. The artesian took one of the head dresses that she had already made that was the exact same colors as Shari's costume, and gave it to her sister Charlene to mail. Now it was a matter of mailing it in time, which can sometimes be challenging in a foreign country.

The head dress came at just the right time for the photo shoot. It is beautifully handcrafted and matches Shari's costume perfectly. This costume was for the cover of her first book, but Shari wanted a fancier costume for her book launch. Her sister ended up buying her the fancier costume for her launch.

Shari's costume is dedicated to all the girls who are still in bondage either physically or emotionally from the past. May all of them find forgiveness and freedom with a bright future filled with hope and love.

 BACKSTORY

We received the head dress within days of the photo shoot and it was the perfect color to go with the costume that her mom had made for her. Check out the cover of Shari's first book, *My Name Is Also Freedom* to see her head dress and full costume.

THE PHOTO SHOOT

Mountains, birds, sunrise...these were all things we were considering for the cover of Shari's autobiography. None of them seemed to completely capture her story except Shari herself. Shari really wanted to wear her costume for the book launch, so we had the idea of having her wear it for the book cover as well. Not only would it represent Shari's life, but it would also represent the lost girls, hidden in the shadows— sold just like she was; the forgotten ones that are still dealing with the aftermath of being sold into slavery.

Once the head dress arrived, Shari had to contact her sister to make sure she was wearing the costume correctly because she did not grow up in the township, and was not sure which way to wear certain parts of her costume. She wanted to make sure to honor her village and represent the tribal girls well. Shari scheduled an appointment to get her make-up done a week before the photo shoot to make sure she liked the way she looked. The photo shoot was important, and she wanted to make sure she looked her best.

The day finally arrived to do her photo shoot and we went to the local department store to get Shari's makeup done. The women were so kind and gave her lots of attention. The lady who did her makeup was very seasoned in the industry, and took great care to make sure her make-up was perfect before she left the store. Shari was treated so kindly and was so beautiful when she left the makeup counter that day.

We left a local department store and started heading north through three different freeways which ended up being almost a three-hour trip! With the air condition on so that Shari's makeup stayed fresh, we finally arrived at the photographer's house for the photo shoot. The photographer was super kind and a friend of my graphic artist, whom I love dearly. It was amazing. We had two professionals on set to make sure we got a great shot for the cover.

Shari changed into her costume, and we took some pictures of her in all black and then some with her costume over it making sure to wear it correctly. The photo shoot was outside by a pool with a lot of different backdrops to choose from. We liked the white and the gold backdrops the best, so we took most of the pictures with those two.

It is important that when Shari goes somewhere she feels comfortable in her environment, so I always check in with her to make sure she is good. Our secret question came up again.

"Do you like her face?" I asked. Code for…do you feel comfortable?

"Yes. I like her face," came Shari's response.

As we progressed throughout the photo shoot, the main question became how much should Shari smile; too much and the book will not seem serious enough. Not enough and it seems too sad. There were many things to think about that day to make sure we got the right picture for her headshot and the perfect cover. The team did a terrific job and the cover speaks for itself! Yet another amazing God story in this whole process of getting her story published.

 BACKSTORY

It took us over three hours on the freeway to get to the photographer's house to shoot the cover, it took us another three hours to get home. Even in all that traffic, it was well worth the drive!

THE HUMAN TRAFFICKING
TASK FORCE #1

Aftercare is critical with human trafficked victims. Once the human trafficked survivor becomes physically free, there are a host of other ways they will need to get free and find hope to continue in their process of healing. Many of the survivors, unfortunately, become trafficked all over again because they do not have any other skills sets for employment, or they do not see their value because of years of abuse. Some know how to read and write, while others were never taught. Each situation is unique for every survivor. Though the situations may be similar at times, the fallout from the abuse can manifest in different ways.

Fortunately, Shari Ho was able to receive help from the Human Trafficking Task Force and all the other different organizations that were part of this amazing task force. One of Shari's caseworkers, Amy Henry, had gone to a Survivor's Caucus. Shari and Amy really wanted to start something similar, so Shari helped brainstorm how they could start a survivor's group with other young ladies who had gone through similar trafficking experiences. Shari began the slow journey of healing. She started to find the help that she needed in these support groups, and eventually Shari became the leader of this group along with another volunteer that had been by her side throughout her ordeal. The Human Trafficking Task Force also had many other services they offered, such as volunteers who would drive Shari to doctor's appointments, counseling appointments, and even simple things such as helping her to get groceries. Because Shari did not have her driver's license at that time, getting rides from volunteers was essential for her.

A volunteer woman from the task force went with Shari and helped her fill out the necessary paperwork to start her own day care business. Owning her own day care has been Shari's dream for many years. As Shari held those babies in her arms and felt their absolute love, God used that experience to show His unconditional love for her. There is something very therapeutic in holding a baby in your arms. This simple act is what God used to restore Shari's spirit as she began to find healing for the very first time. She wants other survivors to experience this healing. Shari's passion is to work with young children and to open a day care in which she can employ human trafficking survivors, along with caring for the children of other survivors.

As the release of Shari's book drew near, the Human Trafficking Task Force invited Shari back to speak at their meeting. She has shared her message with the task force on many occasions over the past fourteen years, but this last time was different. Now at a higher reading level, she was able to read for the first time the bullet points I gave her for her speech, and she could read the notes she had written as well! There are few things greater than watching someone blossom into who they were created to be. Watching her now gain freedom by reading and writing was amazing, and something that most of us take for granted every day.

Shari has been able to share her message with not only the Human Trafficking Task Force but now with other task force groups in the area, and her speaking ability and, most importantly, her confidence is hitting new heights.

A police officer approached her after her presentation at the Human Trafficking Task Force and said, "We go after the perpetrators and it is anger that motivates us to do what we do, but after hearing stories like yours, it is now the love of the survivor that motivates us at a much higher level. You have changed my perspective today."

We are thankful that by sharing her story, Shari has made an impact on people at multiple levels who are involved in rescuing human trafficking victims.

❧ BACKSTORY ☙

A special thank you goes out to all of the people from the Human Trafficking Task Force who went to Taiwan after the Taiwanese government found Shari's family. Their constant involvement and support in Shari's case was invaluable, as she not only navigated seeing her family for the first time in over twenty years, but the especially difficult time in Taiwan when the media followed them around everywhere. Shari is especially grateful to the task force caseworkers who protected her from all the reporters, and constantly fended off the cameras and people pushing to get an interview.

THE ORGANIZATION

Human Trafficking has three main elements: education/ awareness, rescue, and restoration. There are many organizations working on the first elements of education and awareness. Many of these organizations have walk-a-thons throughout the city and other such activities to bring awareness to the issue. I have even heard of an airline stewardess whose campaign was to post toll-free hotline numbers in the bathrooms on airplanes, to alert authorities to possible human-trafficked victims. Many organizations are now posting media ads in airports, bus stations, and other key transitional points.

The second element is the actual rescue of human-trafficked persons with teams of police going in to extract the victims. Not only do they need to rescue the victims, but the police need to make sure it is at an opportune time to take down the traffickers with the most amount of victims they can save. This can be very dangerous work and the effort must be coordinated, with months or sometimes even years in the planning, just to take down one ring of traffickers.

The last element is the restoration piece with teams of people helping the trafficked young women and men once they are free. The restoration piece seems to be the part that is most challenging and forgotten. Many times the young people who are trafficked will go right back into where they came from, because they did not get the help they needed when they got free. The restorative element is not the flashy one that can be shown in the media, but it is the roll-up-your-sleeves and we-are-in-it-for-the-long-run type of job. This is not a short-term program, but years of restorative work with the victims to get them to a place of new normalcy.

There are few organizations that have a strong restoration component to them, in addition to the Human Trafficking Task Force and The Salvation Army. Of the three different parts of this issue, Shari's heart is fully in the restorative part of the journey. For Shari, this is the most important part of the rescue. Her heart is to make sure each victim gets the proper help they need after they have been rescued. She has led human trafficking survivor support groups to help survivors get the help they need through the Human Trafficking Task Force and The Salvation Army. Even in her own need, she leads this group to help others in her same position.

Shari and I decided to fundraise with a non-profit organization called A21 (Abolishing Injustice in the 21st Century) that we felt had a strong restoration component to their organization, in addition to a well-known awareness element that included an international walk-a-thon. My heart has always been with prevention programs and A21 has an amazing curriculum called *Bodies Are Not Commodities*. They have been successful in getting this curriculum into different states in the U.S. and countries all over the world, including South Africa, Australia and Thailand. Since Square Tree Publishing's specialty is curriculum development, and with our team's background in education, this was especially important to us.

We had decided to get more involved with this walk-a-thon and began to fundraise for the event that would take place in a city nearby at the end of the year. The morning arrived and we started early. My alarm went off at 5 a.m. After getting dressed in all black and putting on my running shoes, I drove to pick up Shari at her home, then we drove an hour to the A21 Walk For Freedom event. This is an annual walk they do every year to raise funds and awareness about human trafficking. This was my first time walking in the event, so I did not know what to expect. However, Shari had walked in this event twice before. We were able to meet a lot of A21 staff at the event and find out more about what they do, especially for the survivors, which meant the most to Shari.

There were 500+ people at the event, and I ran into a guy from my church, which was forty miles away. It turns out that he is a small business marketing guy and the perfect person I needed right now with Shari's book launch event coming up. The entire three hours we were there, I kept running into him like divine providence. Even in the pack of 500+ walkers he ended up walking next to us, along with a staff member who was previously a district attorney. Since we were currently in the process of getting Shari's citizenship, she had a connection for us to help us in this process.

"Just show up…with no agenda" is my new motto these days and I am watching what God can do. It is amazing the people He will put around us if we just pay attention to those divine connections.

We walked the boulevard that day with the instructions not to talk. It was a bit eerie to walk without talking, but the effect was great as people stopped to watch us on one of the busiest streets in this huge metropolitan city.

We walked for those that do not yet have the freedom to walk. I would do it again next year!

BACKSTORY

Special thank you to Valerie who works with A21 on their *Bodies Are Not Commodities* curriculum, and for coming along side us and championing Shari to speak at different events.

THE SPEECH COACH

Close to where I live they have a quaint farmer's market that I visited one day with a friend. Out of the corner of my eye, tucked away between the huge zucchini and organic tomatoes, I saw this table with an intriguing sign about human trafficking. I talked to a young lady who turned out to be the founder's daughter who was passing out fliers about their next event. This organization is called the i5 Freedom Network founded by Brenda Wells. Even though the founder was not present, her daughter began to tell me about all the wonderful ways they were training young survivors in the hospitality industry and giving them jobs skills so that they could make a living for themselves. I ended up speaking to Brenda on the phone several days later and found out that she is a trainer for Dale Carnegie classes. Dale Carnegie was an American writer and lecturer and developer of famous self-improvement courses in public speaking and interpersonal skills. He is well-known for his book *How to Win Friends and Influence People*.

I found out that Brenda's organization offered Dale Carnegie training courses, tailored to those having experienced the trauma of human trafficking.

I knew that Shari needed help learning to articulate her story better and to a bigger audience because she was being asked to speak at different events, so I began looking for a speech teacher. When we spoke at the Human Trafficking Task Force meeting, I asked the lady leading the meeting if she knew anyone that could help Shari improve her speaking ability. She mentioned Brenda from the i-5 Freedom Network.

To be honest, I totally forgot that the i-5 Freedom Network offered Dale Carnegie courses, because I was more focused on the training they give to people in the hospitality industry on how to identify and report human trafficking. I called Brenda as soon as I received the referral from the Human Trafficking Task Force to find out when her next Dale Carnegie class was offered. We began a great conversation and determined that Shari really needed one-on-one coaching, and not so much the group coaching. I was thrilled when Brenda offered to do one-on-one training with Shari to get her ready for her new speaking engagements. We set up Shari's first lesson for the following week.

Another answered prayer!

It seemed like God was on overtime answering all our prayer requests and everything we needed to get Shari ready for her book launch and speaking engagements.

The day finally arrived to begin her first lesson. I went flying out of the house that morning, because I was in a hurry to get to Shari's house in time to make our first appointment with her new speech coach. Shari was apprehensive at first, but I told her what I always tell her when we meet someone new in her life—"Let me know if you like her face." This is code for tell me if you feel safe with her. When we got there, Brenda was waiting for us with the PowerPoint presentation I had emailed her of our speech that we had the used last time Shari spoke. She began by having Shari speak for five minutes about her story and then recording it on her phone.

Brenda had a special way she wanted Shari to stand, *Home Base,* she called it. Shari had to learn a new way to stand and project her voice. Then halfway through the session, she closed her laptop, laid aside her agenda and just asked Shari to tell her the whole story of what happened. Through the tears once again, Shari confided in a total stranger the horrific ordeal that she went through as young girl and into her early twenties. Each time I hear Shari tell her story, more details come out that I had not heard before. It is like an onion that with time peels away different layers to her story. When Shari was finished, the coach had exactly what she needed to help Shari become an event speaker.

Brenda began to take the highlight reel of Shari's story and break it down into different parts that were key and drew a picture representing each part of the story on the white board in front of us. There was an incident about Shari being accused of eating The Old Lady's food. The Old Lady put a lock around the refrigerator, so Shari could not get anything out of the refrigerator to eat. She was only allowed to eat leftovers, crouched down on the floor. Brenda drew a picture of a lock to represent this part of the story.

Then there was the part of Shari's story when her dad told her that her mom would come back for her, so Shari sat in a chair at a table with her head down the whole day waiting for her mom to come back. The coach drew a picture of a chair. More pictures were drawn to represent each key highlight of her enslavement.

The pivotal part of Shari's story was the day she made up her mind to call for help. This crucial point in her journey is when The Old Lady's daughter went to the store and asked Shari to pick out some meat. Shari picked the wrong meat at the grocery story. When she got home she got slapped, kicked, thrown to the floor and dragged by her hair—all because she picked the wrong cut of meat. Brenda chose the picture of a pig to represent that fateful day.

By the time the coach was done, she had drawn seven pictures all representing different parts of Shari's story. Because Shari is now learning to improve her reading and writing, drawing pictures was perfect! The coach and I helped Shari craft an introduction statement and a closing statement. The intro and exit statements were the only thing she was supposed to memorize...the rest was 'paint by the numbers,' or 'talk by the pictures.'

Brilliant!

By the time we left, Shari had her full story in pictures and her first homework assignment—memorize the first and last sentence of her speech.

❦ BACKSTORY ❦

After we left our first session with the coach, I asked Shari, "Did you like her face?"

"YES!" came the resounding answer. I knew we would continue seeing Brenda for speech classes.

Emphatic, unequivocal

Loud

THE SPEECH COACH AGAIN

Shari began practicing her speech that she was supposed to have ready for her second lesson with the speech coach. On the drive down to meet Brenda, Shari told me about a Hispanic gentleman that had come to her apartment to help fix her faucet.

When Shari opened the door, he tried to tell her in his broken English that he was there to fix her faucet.

Instead he said, "I fix for me?"

"I help me?" he continued.

Shari heard my voice in her head because of all the times I have corrected her English, in addition to all the lessons she's now been taking at Kumon.

"No, that is not right," she said, as she began instructing him.

"It is not...I fix for *me*...it is, I will fix it for *YOU*," she stated empathically.

"It is not I help *me*...it is, I will help *YOU*," she continued with the same emphasis.

We both roared with laughter realizing that the student had now become the teacher, even though she is still learning at Kumon. She knew enough that what this handyman was trying to say was wrong. Shari was so proud of herself for knowing enough to correct this older gentleman's English.

We pulled up right in time and then we were escorted to the second floor of a beautiful church for her second lesson.

"Did you practice?" Brenda, the speech coach asked.

"Yes," said Shari, even though it was only in the car on the way there!

This time for the lesson we dug into Shari's complex family background and began drawing even more pictures to represent each part of her story. We split her story into three parts. The time she was in Taiwan, then the move to the United States, and lastly when she got free. By the time we were done there were fifteen pictures on the board. At first there were too many pictures to memorize, I thought to myself, but I implicitly trusted Brenda that she knew what she was doing. We then began to break down each part of her story and put an opening sentence and a closing sentence so that Shari would remember. As Shari practiced with these new index cards, the writing was very distracting, so we eventually just went to only the pictures on her cards.

As we dug more into Shari's past, Brenda was struck by the fact that Shari found God in the middle of this abuse by another 'Christian.' It is one of the most inexplicable parts of Shari's story—the fact that she found God in the midst of all the abuse. The Old Lady would take her to church every Sunday, and many times Shari would fall asleep from the sheer exhaustion of the week full of many twenty-hour days. The Old Lady could not do a lot to her in public under the watchful eyes of the congregation members, so sleep came easily. Even though she slept, her spirit was catching the message each week. Teachings about forgiveness and love flooded her mind each Sunday.

The Old Lady and her family were poor examples of the Christian life, yet Shari still found the real true God in the midst of the abuse. What should have been the total opposite in the natural, God turned around in a beautiful way in her life, where she came to lean on Him and look to Him even though it was not always in the traditional religious or church way.

There have been many people who have asked, "Is Shari really a Christian?" which is completely off base. Nothing could be further from the truth, because she had to rely on him every day.

They ask this because the way she found God was not traditional—not with a Bible in one arm while going to a life group every week. Shari's love for God was pure, yet simple. A true love for Him. No rules, just pure love.

147

During this speech class, we discussed the many different ways her sisters had responded to their own challenging circumstances. Each sister handled their situation in a different manner, but somehow Shari found God and that made all the difference for her. She eventually learned how to forgive her mom and dad and learned to let go of the anger of her situation. She learned even more about her faith once she was freed.

Shari is a real example of pure, simple faith.

"Blessed are the pure in heart,
for they shall see God."

—Matthew 5:8

 BACKSTORY

In my past I have 'made things happen', but now God was sending me amazing people to work with us and I did not have to go and 'make anything happen.' God was doing it all on His own. I am continuing to learn every day to lay down my own agenda, because God's agenda is so much better!

THE PLANNING MEETING

What started as a simple small intimate book launch for Shari, has grown into a major human trafficking event where Shari will be the keynote speaker. The name of the event is—*Freedom Has a Name.* I knew I needed help, so I began calling some of my friends who worked with human trafficking ministries to come to my house for a dinner meeting to begin planning this huge event. What started with a couple friends swelled to eight with one that could not make it. The funny thing is that I was more worried about what I would cook for dinner, than the meeting itself.

The caliber of these friendships and the level of maturity and wisdom each of them brought to the table confirmed I had made the right decision in selecting this particular group. They brought integrity and care for the victims of human trafficking, yet had the experience in working with them to know what they truly needed. They cared about getting the word out there and to bring awareness to such a dark place.

In addition to their wisdom, they had a rolodex full of people they knew that I could contact. People from all different industries and organizations that could help. By the end of the night, I had tons of contacts to follow up with, and I was able to use their name as a reference.

At the end of the evening, everyone left and I was excited, yet a bit overwhelmed. Yes, they had given me their contacts and many great ideas, but what I realized after they left is that I failed to delegate any of the tasks needed to put on such a big event. After they left, I felt very overwhelmed.

The next day, I reached out to one of my friends, the gal who was not able to make it to the meeting. We met a few days later at a local restaurant. I updated her on the meeting and all the ideas that were circulated. Then the big God reveal came.

A few years ago, there was a big event at our church called the Freedom Event. I remember going to it and being impressed with how many different organizations were there as well as the participants who attended. What I did not know was my friend was one of the directors of the event as well as another friend who came to my meeting at my house!

My friend went on to explain how she and my other friend got people to the event and had 750 attendees the first year and over 1,200 the second year...even though it rained on the day of the event!

God showed up yet again. I did not feel alone doing the event anymore, and now I had someone with the experience and track record to back it up.

My friend and I began dreaming about what we wanted the event to look like. We ended up staying so late at the restaurant that the entire section we were sitting in closed except for the two of us sitting in the back. We had that whole section to ourselves to dream, create, and visualize the event. By the time I left three hours later, we had a plan. She remained at the restaurant putting more ideas together after I left. What a complete godsend she has been. I no longer felt alone, and I now had the confidence with her at the helm to help me.

BACKSTORY

Fun fact…I had been 'babysitting' my friend's furniture for eight months prior to our meeting at my house. Three days before everyone was coming to my dinner meeting, my friend needed her furniture back which completely wiped out my living room. I knew everyone was coming over, so I scrambled to put some six-foot tables together and placed them in the center of our huge living room. Problem solved, and no one even knew I did not have any furniture!

THE HUMAN TRAFFICKING
TASK FORCE #2

Shari and I were invited to speak at another local Human Trafficking Task Force monthly meeting. She had already spoken at the other task force meeting, so I had a benchmark of her speaking abilities only four weeks earlier. With three speech sessions behind her, Shari was ready for her first speaking event with her newfound skills. Her speech teacher gave her index cards with pictures on each of them, reminding Shari of the different parts of her story. It was not only a great way to keep track of her story, but we had chosen the most poignant parts to highlight so that she remembered them standing behind the podium.

Shari's story is emotionally heavy, so after we selected some of her memories to highlight, I suggested we tell the story of the dog. In the midst of all this abuse, there was one 'person' that showed her love, and that was The Old Lady's dog.

Shari would brush out the dog's thick coat, feed it, and pick up after it. That dog loved her!

It was a beautiful but high energy husky who loved to chew on things. His favorite thing to chew on was shoes. Every day the family would find a shoe that he had snuck out of the bedroom and hid in the corner of the family room to chew on, hidden from the owner's view. The Old Lady's daughter used to yell at the dog because he chewed up her very expensive sandals.

But that dog never chewed Shari's shoes…EVER!

Shari only had one pair of shoes, so if the dog chewed her shoes she would not have another pair to wear. God had graciously sent this big slobbering bundle of love into Shari's life for a reason and showed her that He cared for her by having the dog refrain from chewing up her only pair of shoes.

As her speech coach worked with Shari on her speech, we thought putting this story in the middle would lighten the heaviness of her story. So as Shari came up to speak, I was waiting to see how the audience would react to the dog story and if it had the intended affect by putting some humor and lightening Shari's story a bit. As Shari began to tell the story of the dog and her shoes, the audience laughed while at the same time crying. I have never seen anything like this before.

As an audience member myself I understood. You wanted to laugh, but you also knew the grim reality of the situation, so you laughed while at the same time it made you cry. It was powerful beyond words. Later she told the story of her rescuer, Judy, who on the night she had escaped, took her to eat and then went immediately to a local department store to buy her a pair of shoes. Buying anything for herself was a new experience for Shari. Judy asked her what size she wore, but she had no idea, so Judy had Shari stand on the cold metal shoe measuring device to find out what size she was. Size 5 is her shoes size!

The shoe story had now come full circle in her speech. Shoes represent such a simple life need that we take for granted, and yet Shari was denied owning more than one pair of hand-me-down shoes for years.

Shari continued her speech with varied memories of her harrowing journey, all the while profusely thanking the police department and special agents for helping to save her that night she escaped. She went on to talk about forgiveness and how forgiving the people that have hurt her has set her free. Then she came to this final line in her speech.

"Judy gave me my physical freedom, but God gave me my emotional freedom."

The crowd erupted with claps and stood to their feet in an overwhelming standing ovation.

I felt like a proud mama as I stood to my feet and clapped until my hands turned red as tears streamed down my face like everyone else in the room.

During Shari's speech, she thanked the police and special agents. She said that she wanted to meet one of the agents that helped her through this ordeal. I had been trying to find this particular agent and had called the local police departments for several weeks, but no one seemed to know him. Melodie, the author of Shari's first book, wanted to interview him but was never able to find him either. I was finally able to find out that he worked for Homeland Security, but I had not followed up to track him down at that office yet. I wanted Shari to be able to meet the Federal Agent to thank him in person.

BACKSTORY

After Shari was finished speaking, in the middle of her standing ovation, a woman from the audience came up to the microphone and said, I work for Homeland Security and I work with this agent. I have already contacted him and he wants to meet you! I stood there completely amazed and shocked at what had just happened.

Many times on this journey of writing Shari's story, I have felt like I am walking into something much bigger than myself, Shari, or any other assignment I have partnered with God on.

All I can say is…do it again, God…do it again!

THE FEDERAL AGENT

"I called the agent and he is excited to meet Shari," the female Homeland Security officer said at the task force meeting.

"Okay," was all I could stammer, completely shocked at what just happened.

Shari and I finished the meeting and I went back to my office. I had totally forgotten to get the agent's contact information. In my shock, I did not ask for it.

I looked on the internet to find his number, but to no avail. All I could find was a general number with only an automated recording for general information.

I sent the female Homeland Security officer an email and then waited anxiously to get her response. What seemed like days of emails going back and forth, I finally received an email from this agent.

I had introduced myself to him in the email and explained how Shari wanted to meet with him. Another week went by while we were getting approvals from his department so that we could meet. Then the day finally came.

We met in a private club house so that no one would overhear the confidential nature of the conversation. We each came with gifts for each other and exchanged pleasantries. Shari was so excited to thank him personally for all he had done for her.

The last time Shari had seen this agent was fourteen years ago when he was just getting married. Now with his hair greying, this amazing man recounted the events surrounding her rescue.

Throughout the conversation, tears welled up in the agent's eyes as we instinctively knew that this case was different from other cases that he had worked on in the past. He had even kept a portion of the files and pictures, even though over a decade had past.

The night Shari was rescued, there was a local sheriff's deputy that spoke to her through an interpreter. Shari was hiding in a closet so that the police would not take her back to The Old Lady's house. The deputy found her in the closet and asked her to come out. She came out and fell on the ground and grabbed his feet, begging him not to take her back to The Old Lady. The Homeland Security Agent said there was also a local detective initially working the case and that he would try to locate him for us.

We spoke for what seemed like minutes although a couple hours had gone by. In addition to thanking him, Shari emphasized the importance that law enforcement should help the victims. Many of them are not ready to testify or even feel safe or emotionally secure enough to do this right away when they get free. Help is needed in that transition time. The victims may feel confused about their captors or brainwashed, sometimes not wanting to hurt their perpetrators in anyway. He listened very intently, and you could tell he cared deeply, especially about Shari's case.

As our visit came to a close, none of us wanted it to end. This emotional 'reunion' in the most unlikely manner of bringing these two together was another one of God's gift to Shari.

 BACKSTORY

The Homeland Security Agent spoke with a detective who was initially part of the investigation, but he was unable to locate the deputy—the one who helped Shari that night, when she fell at his feet, begging not to be sent back to The Old Lady's house. We are still looking for him.

THE UNIVERSITY

"Oh...God! I need a venue for Shari's event!" I said in more of a moan than a prayer.

"It is coming. I have this!" I felt the Lord gently say to me.

"When Lord...when?" I questioned. Nothing notable came.

I continued to ask different people who came across my path, but still no venue. I pressed in and kept going while keeping the faith that the venue would come.

Shari kept insisting that I connect with Congressman Ed Royce. She had met him several times and really liked him. He was kind and helpful and considerate to her every time she met with him, and he also had a heart for human-trafficked victims. Shari began asking me each time we met if I had called him yet. I kept telling her I did not have the time to call him. The truth was that I was a bit afraid to cold-call a

Congressman. I was not sure what would happen. But finally, Shari's voice in my head kept haunting me.

"Okay," I thought to myself.

"What is the worst thing that can happen...they just do not take my call?" I continued with my reasoning.

I dialed the phone and the receptionist answered.

"I would like to talk to the congressman's assistant please," I stammered.

Shortly a sweet voice came on the line and I told her who I was and that I was working with Shari Ho.

"Oh...I remember her!" she said all excited.

This was a good sign, I thought. I continued to tell her about our needs for a venue and she said she would look into it and let me know what she could do. She mentioned two universities that she thought would be a great fit for the event, and she would get back in touch with me later.

I waited and followed up for weeks which turned into months. I was still concerned because we did not have a venue, and I needed to put together the invitations and have people register for the event. I decided to take matters into my own hands and instead of waiting, went to other places looking for a venue, but thankfully they did not work out.

After a couple months, we found out that one of the universities was interested in hosting the event. It took many weeks to go through the proper channels to see if we got the final approval, and then we found out that we did. I was thrilled because this university was my alma mater and one of my favorite universities out of the two that I graduated from. I had always loved that campus because it was big for a university, but not too big that you feel lost on campus.

The day finally arrived for me to look at the venue on campus. The dean was amazing and showed me around and took me on a tour of the theater they had in mind for us. It was a nice theater, but it just did not sit right in my spirit. I felt like there had to be more.

The lady who gave us a tour of the theater asked, "Do you want to come in through the newly built theater entrance and come around to this theater?"

"What newly built theater?" I asked with curiosity.

"The one over there," she pointed around the corner.

"May I go and see that one?" I asked cautiously, wanting to seem still grateful for what they offered.

"Yes, we can walk over there," she said not bothered by the request.

Off we went to this stunningly beautiful theater. She said she was not sure if the theater was available on the date that we wanted. After I left the campus, I graciously prayed that God would help us get that theater.

The name of the theater is called the Meng theater. It is apropos that the theater has a Chinese name. Meng means energetic which is very much Shari's personality.

Days went by as I kept praying for this theater. Then the email came from the dean…

"We got the theater!" The dean wrote in a very short email.

"Details to follow," she continued.

Again…we had to wait. Wait to see what the details were and what costs would be associated with this magnificent place. Now my attention turned to…how in the world were we going to fill an 800-seat theater?

You would think by now my faith was soaring with all we had been through, but my thoughts went to how we were going to fill the theater. I had to learn to trust God through every step of this process, even though I could not always see the next step. God had been faithful every turn of this four-and-a-half-year journey with Shari. He was not about to stop now.

⊷⧉ BACKSTORY ⧉⊶

I had felt in my heart for some reason that we needed the event to be on January 19th, although I couldn't tell you why I felt that way. There were other places that offered us a venue on different dates, but it never seemed right. Then Melodie, the writer of Shari's autobiography, was doing some research and watch the video of Shari landing in the airport to see her family for the first time since she was free. Melodie looked down at the timestamp on the video and it said January 19th! That was exactly seven years to the day that Shari stepped foot in Taiwan with her freedom!

THE CITIZENSHIP JOURNEY

"**D**o you know anywhere I can go to help Shari get her U.S. Citizenship?" I asked several people.

"No, we only know where to get the U.S. Visa," they said.

Most of the people I reached out to did not know the process to get U.S. Citizenship. When Shari got free, there was a team of amazing people from the Human Trafficking Task Force that worked diligently to help her get permanent residency in the United States. Now that she had been free for over ten years, it was time to take the next step and help her get her U.S. Citizenship so that when she traveled all over the world, we would have it.

My break came at the planning committee meeting I had at my house. One of the ladies had a contact with Legal Aide and gave me the lawyer's contact phone number, who happened to also go to our church. I tried several times to reach her, and what seemed like telephone tag on steroids led me like a huge jigsaw puzzle in finding the right person to help us. My contact led me to the legal team that works with the city's libraries newly formed New Americans Initiative section.

I called the general number and you could not really leave a message, but the voicemail said to press pound to get a directory if you knew the person's name you wanted to call. My business skills came into full swing as I typed in common names of people to see if I could find anyone to talk to on the phone.

"S...u...e...," I typed in the phone, but no one by that name.

"J...o...h...n...," I typed on the keyboard.

I hit the jackpot when I got the voicemail of a young man who worked there and left his cell phone number to reach him. I sent him a text and he responded within the hour.

Leaving nothing to chance I called back again and tried some more common English names and found another gal and left a voicemail with her, too. The young man only had openings during the week, but suggested I sign up for their next consultation at the Saturday workshop they were having. I did not really want to make the long drive on my birthday, but if that is what it would take then I would do it.

The next day I received a call from Marilyn, the woman with whom I left a message. I totally forgot I had left her a message as well. She was amazing and filled in all the missing pieces I needed to know about becoming a U.S. Citizen. Shari was scared of taking the test to become a U.S. Citizen and that is why she never fully pursued it. Instinctively, I knew it would be a long process and that we needed to start the paperwork now.

After questioning the woman about the whole process, I was correct that it would take a year to get her citizenship. Marilyn was gracious enough to walk me through the entire process and all the paperwork I would need to bring with Shari the day we came to the meeting. I felt more at ease about the process and found out that the test was not as stringent as we thought.

Then I received another email from a lawyer specializing in naturalization, and she offered to meet with us on a Saturday only fifteen minutes from the house. We ended up taking her up on the offer, and after three hours, Shari is now in the process of becoming a U.S. Citizen.

God knows just how to time everything perfectly if we just let go and trust Him through the process. In divine providence, the manager of Kumon had called me a couple weeks earlier and said he wanted to increase the time Shari comes into their tutoring center. He wanted her to come in four days a week so that she would continue to progress in the English language and her reading and writing skills. Shari was ready to quit Kumon because it was just too much homework, and with the book launch approaching fast, it was a bit overwhelming for her. The manager of Kumon and I made her a deal. If she came four days a week to Kumon, then she did not have to do her homework. That was the deal that turned Shari back towards Kumon. Little did we know at the time, this is EXACTLY what she would need to take the U.S. Citizenship test. Part of the U.S. Citizenship testing process is writing and reading sentences in English.

 BACKSTORY

We are still in process, but God's perfect timing has always amazed me. The manager of Kumon calling at the exact time we needed Shari to progress faster through her English lessons in order to take this test was complete divine providence.

THE NEW BEGINNING

When I first met Shari, she had been free almost ten years, yet the pain of her enslavement was still affecting her every day. Each time I met with her, there were many tears recounting her time being a slave. Each story described in detail the pain she experienced and seemed recent, like she had just gotten free. It took one full year before she fully trusted me and agreed to allow us to tell her story. There were many people during those ten years that offered to publish her story, especially when the media firestorm hit, but Shari never felt it was the right fit.

Once she began trusting me, I introduced her to Melodie, Square Tree's content editor, who would write her autobiography, *My Name is Also Freedom*. I knew that Melodie was the right person to tell her story because she is very thorough in her approach, and one of her strengths is to capture the voice of the author and not use her own voice. The challenging thing about Shari is that she is many different people wrapped into one. She has some Taiwanese culture, along with Chinese culture, while at the same time having an indigenous tribe culture. Take all those cultures, mix it with the United States, and be a survivor, and you have a very complex, blended person. Melodie was ready to take on the challenge. It took Melodie three and a half years after I introduced her to Shari, and over 40 interviews later, including a trip to Taiwan, to put the story together.

There were many times Shari asked me, "Is the book done yet?" I felt the frustration in her voice.

"It's coming soon," I would always tell her to encourage her.

"I cannot wait! I have dreamt about this day for a very long time," she would often say.

"Me too," I would say, hoping Melodie would be finished soon.

To be honest, I was just as frustrated as Shari was because I felt like it was taking so long, yet now looking back I would not have it any other way!

Shari has grown tremendously in the last four-and-a-half years. Telling her story takes the pain out of it, and each time she tells it, she finds a little more healing. There are less tears with each retelling. There were new memories that surfaced in these past four years. Memories that she had either buried or forgotten, but with each new memory she was able to face it and find forgiveness in the process.

The greatest level of healing, however, came when she went back to Taiwan and faced those dark places where she was held captive. Shari had been back to Taiwan several times since she was free, but this time was different.

Surrounded by loving and supportive friends, she was able to go back to those dark places and find emotional freedom from the past. Some days on the trip she was very quiet and simply processing the pain and the emotions of the past and then working through it. On those quiet days, we supported her and let her process and find healing. She has been completely transformed and is a different person from the young lady I met many years ago.

This quote reminds me of Shari's life.

> *"You're here to be light, bringing out the God-colors in the world. God is not a secret to be kept. We're going public with this, as public as a city on a hill...Now that I've put you there on a hilltop, on a light stand—shine! Keep open house; be generous with your lives. By opening up to others, you'll prompt people to open up with God, this generous Father in heaven."*
>
> —Matthew 5:14-16 (MSG)

We have grown close in these four-and-a-half years, and I look at her as my daughter, although I am not old enough to be her mother. There are many times I have given her that 'mom' look or gone with her to the drugstore to buy her some medicine, or even brought her chicken soup when she was not feeling well. I have this innate sense to take care of her. It has been an amazing journey and she has blessed me as much as I have blessed her. Shari is a very special young lady that God is going to use to bring out the God-colors in the world in a big way.

Since the very first day I met her she has grown tremendously. God has been preparing her all these years for this new season of speaking, publishing her books, and possibly a movie—who knows what this next God-adventure is going to bring. But this is for sure, if our trip to Taiwan was any indication of what is to come, it will be the best God-adventure of a lifetime!

It is an honor and an absolute pleasure walking this journey alongside her and the Square Tree team. It has not been an easy journey, but then nothing is easy in life when it is worth it. I pray that these God-stories have not only inspired you, but that they have given you a greater level of faith for your own life. I know that is what Shari would want for you, too.

"Always be patient; endure and overcome
because tomorrow will always be better."
—Shari Ho's mother told
Shari the night she was sold

Shari Ho's Story

My Name Is Also Freedom

Available on Amazon

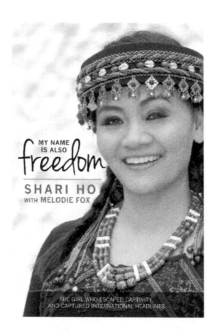

"This story goes deeper into the heart and humanity that binds law enforcement with those whom we protect."
                    —Special Agent, Homeland Security Investigations

"I love that this book showcases both Shari's compassion for others and her incredible sense of justice. She has an important voice and I am so glad to have gotten to observe her become *Shari*."

—Amy Henry
Former case manager and Anti-Trafficking
Director, The Salvation Army

"...My heart was pounding so loud I could feel the blood pulsing in my ears. Every nerve was on alert. Did I hear someone behind me? I rolled the garbage cans to the curb, like I did every Thursday night in this wealthy community, the only task I did unattended, a brief moment away from the watchful eyes of my captors, those I had been sold a slave to when I was just seven years old in Taiwan. Now was my chance to escape. I bolted, running as fast as I could towards the end of the street and into the car that was waiting for me. Everything I owned I left behind, except the tattered shirt and dirty pants I wore, clothes that reminded me of the life I had been living these past twenty years—a torn and ravaged existence, a victim of human trafficking..."

Shari Ho's incredible story of slavery and survival to inspirational speaker will grip your soul and challenge you to speak up on behalf of the silent ones around you, those who long to say.... "My Name is Also Freedom."

"Shari Ho's story was as heartbreaking to learn as it was compelling to read about. Melodie Fox retold her experience and found Shari's voice with a straight forward sort of compassion that managed to convey the horrific reality while showing her undeniable resilience. Shari's life as a slave to a heartless and calculating Old Lady was not enough to destroy her spirit and faith in God. Through the tears I felt hope. And just as I was feeling disappointed in all those who could have helped Shari during her desperate journey, I was inspired by those who ultimately stepped in and committed themselves to her freedom. A non-stop read, Melodie Fox channeled the inner voice of Shari such that you felt like you were there alongside her, trapped, enraged, hopeful, free.

This book is a must-read for anyone looking to understand more about the reality and dynamics of modern-day slavery."

—Brenda Wells, Founder i-5 Freedom Network

For more information www.shariho.com.

Available on AMAZON.

If you see something that is suspicious
report it immediately!

National Human Trafficking Hotline
888-373-7888

SQUARE TREE PUBLISHING

At **SQUARE TREE PUBLISHING**, we believe your message matters. That is why our dedicated team of professionals is committed to bringing your literary texts and targeted curriculum to a global marketplace. We strive to make that message of the highest quality, while still maintaining your voice. We believe in you, therefore, we provide a platform through website design, blogs, and social media campaigns to showcase your unique message. Our innovative team offers a full range of services from editing to graphic design inspired with an eye for excellence, so that your message is clearly and distinctly heard.

Whether you are a new writer needing guidance with each step of the process, or a seasoned writer, we will propel you to the next level of your development.

At **SQUARE TREE PUBLISHING**, it's all about **you**.

Take advantage of a free consultation.

Your opportunity is "Write Outside the Box"!

www.SquareTreePublishing.com

Made in the USA
San Bernardino, CA
30 December 2018